Including LGBT Parented Families in Schools

T0315411

This book explores the experiences of LGBTQ+ parented families in school communities and provides a voice for this overlooked group who are becoming an increasingly common form of family diversity in school communities.

Approaching the topic from a strength-based psychological perspective, the book presents LGBTQ+ parents' suggestions for school improvements and supportive structures and provides empirical evidence to inform future LGBTQ+ inclusive education policy.

Research-based yet practically focused, it will be a valuable resource for researchers, students and education professionals alike.

Trent Mann is a casual academic and PhD student in the School of Education at Macquarie University currently lecturing in postgraduate educational psychology units, and a range of educational subjects. His research explores developmental psychology, educational sociology, community health research, inter-disciplinary approaches to research, educational policy and mixed-method research designs with a focus on LGBTQ+ groups in school communities (students, parents/guardians and school staff). Trent was awarded the Faculty of Human Sciences Thesis Excellence Award for his Masters of Research exploring LGBTQ+ parents' experiences in Australian school contexts (Mann & Jones).

Tiffany Jones is a Professor in the School of Education at Macquarie University who researches LGBTIQ+ issues in education, education policy, health and social policy. Her peer-reviewed books include new releases *Improving Services for Transgender and Gender Variant Youth*, *A Student-centred Sociology of Education: Voices of Experience*, *Uplifting Gender and Sexuality Education Research* and *Bent Street vol. 5.1*. Professor Jones liaises and constructs technical, policy and data reports with UN bodies and sits on the editorial board of the peer-reviewed academic journals *Sex Education*, *LGBT Health* and *LGBT Youth*, and edits *Bent Street*.

Including LGBT Parented Families in Schools

Research to Inform Policy and Practice

Trent Mann and Tiffany Jones

Routledge
Taylor & Francis Group

LONDON AND NEW YORK

First published 2022
by Routledge
2 Park Square, Milton Park, Abingdon, Oxon OX14 4RN

and by Routledge
605 Third Avenue, New York, NY 10158

Routledge is an imprint of the Taylor & Francis Group, an informa business

© 2022 Trent Mann and Tiffany Jones

The right of Trent Mann and Tiffany Jones to be identified as authors of this work has been asserted in accordance with sections 77 and 78 of the Copyright, Designs and Patents Act 1988.

Trademark notice: Product or corporate names may be trademarks or registered trademarks, and are used only for identification and explanation without intent to infringe.

British Library Cataloguing-in-Publication Data
A catalogue record for this book is available from the British Library

Library of Congress Cataloging-in-Publication Data
A catalog record has been requested for this book

ISBN: 978-0-367-76501-9 (hbk)
ISBN: 978-0-367-76500-2 (pbk)
ISBN: 978-1-003-16747-1 (ebk)

DOI: 10.4324/9781003167471

Typeset in Times New Roman
by codeMantra

Contents

1 Introducing LGBTQ+ parents in media, culture & education policy

LGBTQ+ parents reflect on: how others construct them?

My sons are afraid of being bullied and teased in school if anyone sees their 'trans' parent.

(Josephine, 43 yrs, South Australia)

I took my girlfriend to my daughter's sports carnival and got dirty looks from parents and teachers. I would be more willing to do these things if I felt more welcome.

(Bella, 33 yrs, Queensland)

...teachers are often shocked or unsure with how to react when learning that my children have two mothers.

(Evelyn, 27 yrs, Queensland)

As a parent who is transgender, despite 50/50 care, my children's schools and teachers do not tend to regard me as an equal parent, assuming perhaps that I have less input or custody.

(Jordan, 42 yrs, South Australia)

1.1 Introduction

Individuals, couples and extended groups of parents who may identify as or include people of Lesbian, Gay, Bisexual, Trans, and other sexual orientations and gender identities (LGBTQ+) have become a global 'hot topic'. Their controversiality has especially increased with their expanding coverage in the news media, representation in popular culture and manifestation within political/legislative debates as a growing number of countries have legalised recognition of gender transition, marriage equality and alternate family structures in the last two decades. Such representation and recognition are not unproblematic goods, and may shape and misinform assumptions about

DOI: 10.4324/9781003167471-1

LGBTQ+ people in schools – which LGBTQ+ parents themselves describe in the opening reflections as often absent or negative given a dearth of quality educational material. Further, whilst changes in legislative frameworks are intended to offer LGBTQ+ parents the same legal recognition, protection and rights as heterosexual parents, there has been significant debate around 'if and how' these amendments in laws should be recognised – and duly, reflected – in schools. However, the key debates and research studies in the area generally fail to include the thoughts and opinions of LGBTQ+ parents themselves, and may indeed also be based on assumptions stemming from less relevant contextual sources and phenomena. Particularly, how LGBTQ+ parents would (and/or would *not*) like to be included or represented within school contexts, is an unexplored terrain that needs to be considered.

This book addresses such needs by offering educational professionals, policy makers, pre-service educators, advocates/allies, researchers and parents an insightful guide into LGBTQ+ parents' perspectives – foregrounding their own voices and experiences. It provides overviews of the historical development of LGBTQ+ parent research, research exploring the experiences of LGBTQ+ parents in social contexts, LGBTQ+ parents' experiences in their child's school environments, and parents' views on how schools can be improved to create more welcoming and inclusive learning environments. This introductory chapter briefly considers the evolving nature of LGBTQ+ parent constructions in three key public realms, to better understand the context for their construction within education and research. First, it considers the representation of LGBTQ+ parents in the public media. Second, it examines the representation of LGBTQ+ parents in popular culture. Finally, it looks at LGBTQ+ rights in policies and highlights various issues in policy and education as key gaps for research and a central concern addressed in the book.

1.2 News media 'factual' constructions of LGBTQ+ parents

The increasing visibility of LGBTQ+ parents in the news media around the world can, in partial ways, reflect the public struggles and views around LGBTQ+ parents with immediacy. Given a dearth of alternate information upon LGBTQ+ parents for school communities (see Josephine and Evelyn's reflections in the opening chapter), media may be some education stakeholders' first known exposure to them. Thus media on LGBTQ+ parents can be fundamentally educational for viewers on these minorities' social value or lack thereof, whether or not intended (Kahn, 2014). This includes media debates about families, where representations of LGBTQ+ parents can be used by the media to challenge delegitimising claims about queer families and seek to defend queer parenthood or, at times, to reinforce hetero-gendered norms (Carlile & Paechter, 2018; Lynch & Morison, 2016; Nguyen, 2015).

Particular LGBTQ+ parent celebrities are the figures who most strongly and repeatedly feature in Western media representations within and even across different countries, in ways that afford different constructions of LGBTQ+ parenting. Perhaps most notably gay fathers Elton John and David Furness in the United Kingdom (UK); Ricky Martin and Jwan Yosef, or Matt Bomer and Neil Patrick Harris, or B.D. Wong in the United States (US) are used to provide an image of a luxurious, well-resourced and creative parenting lifestyle (Carlile & Paechter, 2018; Kahn, 2014; Lynch & Morison, 2016). Trans mother Caitlyn Jenner, lesbian mother Melissa Etheridge and bisexual mother Madonna in the US have been used to provide pictures of rebellious strong women mothering in their own unique way(s) in and out of relationships, against much backlash.

News media coverage on everyday non-celebrity LGBTQ+ parents also contributes to their constructions of the group. Carlile and Paechter (2018) explored representations of LGBTQ+ parents in UK newspapers, finding that most media articles in a year focussed on lesbian mothers (74), then gay fathers (42), then bisexual parents (23). There were only five representations of transgender parents and no representations of broader LGBT, queer, intersex, or polyamorous parents. Dominant constructions included 'the evil lesbian mother' engaged in witchcraft, hypnosis and deception – distinguishing 'the biological mother' as bewitched by 'her lesbian lover' in tales of murder, torture or online grooming. This may in part be attributed to the privileging of titillating constructions of women in UK media broadly, known for its 'page 3 girls', which lesbians can be worked into exploitatively. There was the 'acceptable LGBTQI+ parent' marked by their wealth, consumer power and aristocracy – usually males like sperm donor Ivan Massow hosting his pregnant lesbian recipient after her breakup, in which wealth was a valorising factor, tandem to the coverage of Elton and David. Acceptance by family members was often remarked upon, and there were constructions of authors as being 'confused' by the 'complexity' of (simple) LGBTQ+ parenting arrangements.

Lynch and Morison explored resistant discourses deployed in South African mainstream print media, attending particularly to news reports about queer fathers (Lynch & Morison, 2016). Through a critical thematic analysis of 152 South African newspaper articles over a 30-year period, informed by feminist discursive psychology, they reinforced the finding that most media articles over a 30-year period focussed on lesbian mothers (45.4%), and then gay fathers (25.2%). Considerably fewer articles considered bisexual, transgender or intersex parents (1.3%). Dominant constructions included 42% of articles focussing on 'Struggle stories (custody struggles; legal battles; rights)'; 18.4% on 'General queer marriage and family'; 12.5% on 'Parenting, child development, and "effects" on children'; and 11.2% on 'Testimonies/experiences of parents and/or their children'. Smaller portions considered means towards becoming LGBTQ parents with 7.9% of articles exploring 'Assisted reproductive technologies (e.g. surrogacy; IVF)' and 4.6% on 'Adoption or foster care'. Compared to the UK, a much smaller portion focussed on 'Bad parenting (child abuse/harm/murder)' (2.6%).

In Australia, media discussion of LGBTQ+ parents has centred around marriage equality debates in the decade preceding the 2017 marriage plebiscite and supposedly controversial resources in schools depicting LGBTQ+ parents such as *Gayby Baby*. A strong trope from both right and left coverage of these themes included arguments on 'the best interests of the child' of potentially married LGBTQ+ parents (Cubby, 2004; Hook, 2017; Tomazin, 2016; Von Doussa & Power, 2019). LGBTQ+ families with children were mentioned in around a fifth of Australian newspaper articles in 2013 and in the years before the same-sex marriage plebiscite (Nguyen, 2015). In these debates, parents most especially including long-time political figure and lesbian mother Penny Wong, could be sometimes featured as stable, calmly quiet and no-nonsense coupled providers in ways that reinforced arguments about LGBTQ+ parents as being able to support children's best interests. 'Model' Australian LGBTQ+ parents therefore were put forth to support broader rights policy pushes to which children's disinterests played a significant psycho-social threat in the collective mind of the Australian populous. Wong's impassioned response to negations of marriage equality as serving childrens' best interests was often quoted in media at the time; 'what you're saying to not just me but people like me is that the most important thing in our lives, which is the people we love, is somehow less good, less valued' (Nguyen, 2015, p. 296).

Australian public health scholar and lesbian mother Jennifer Powers was repeatedly asked to write or talk about whether kids with Queer parents were damaged compared to other kids in this period (Von Doussa & Power, 2019, p. 53):

Usually it is being asked by people on the ultra-right who want ammunition to vilify gay people, to prove they should not be allowed to have kids. Or, people want a defense against the ultra-right – 'the kids are okay, look the science proves it!' Really, if they thought the kids were not doing well they might be asking what they could do to better support kids who have queer parents, not asking whether or not they should have been born (…) They can't directly critique adults' right to be gay, so anti-gay campaigners have to find these other issues to mount their attack – usually they find a way in through the idea they are just protecting children. But I don't think they are protecting anyone.

Powers reflected that divorce/separation is another ground on which protection of children is raised, and being a lesbian parent forced her to be 'out' in education environments about being divorced and entering new relationships with women – merely to explain the needs of her children. She thus experienced some alienation from dominant LGBTQ+ parent 'marriage equality' media narratives, the ideal 'homo-nuclear family' model the left relied on and its appeals to normativity. Australian sociologist and bisexual mother Genine Hook similarly argued queer figures' promotion of same-sex marriage as 'in the best interests of the child' during marriage equality debates created an implicit and highly problematic attack on solo queer parents in the media, including herself (Hook, 2017). She described experiencing a loss of valued access to Queer theoretical arguments contesting heteronormative privileging of coupled parents above the full rich diversity of parenting experiences, through Queer's realignment with and overemphasis on 'coupling norms' in the press. Solo parents, divorced parents, racial/ethnic diversity, polyamory, extended families and other variation from the privileged construction were excluded from the media-sanitised 'facts'. Diversities within diversity are considered 'too much', messing up simplistic 'best interests' LGBTQ+ parenting constructions – thus, even ostensibly 'positive' media on LGBTQ+ parents offer education stakeholders only *partial* truths and depictions.

Lynch and Morison identified four themes in resistant ways of talking about LGBTQ+ parents in the South African media (Lynch & Morison, 2016):

- de-gendering parenthood,
- normalising queer parents,
- valorising queer parenting, and
- challenging the heteronormative gold standard.

Considering Hook and Powers' experiences, we should remember that parenthood can be de-gendered and de-coupled in media representation so that genderqueer parents' contributions to child-rearing can be more fully appreciated, and that any individual parent's contributions whether solo, in a couple, or in other parenting arrangements can be more fully appreciated and contextualised without limitations on how parents may support their child in social/financial/domestic and other ways considered 'masculine', 'feminine' or otherwise... so that ultimately children can be seen as potentially fully supported by different types of guardians in their worlds. Similarly, normalising and valorising queer parents could be more widely distributed across the intersections of identity... moving away from only valuing wealthy coupled gay males and towards encouraging representations of other LGBTQ+ parents from across spectrums of social classes, genders, race/ethnicity demographics and relationship experiences. These representations may more squarely challenge the cis/heteronormative standard as the 'gold', against which homonormativity begs its 'silver'.

Overall, LGBTQ+ parents' preferences for how they are treated and represented occur not in a vacuum but in the context of – and potential response to – media constructions shaping how other school stakeholders imagine and receive them. Both the earlier and ongoing media constructions of LGBTQ+ parents as 'bad' rebels and problematic deviants potentially harming the interests of their children, and the more recent constructions of well-resourced coupled providers offering lifestyles reminiscent of cis-gendered heteronormative parenting in the 'best interests of children', provide difficult headlines for LGBTQ+ parents to contrast against when engaging with schools.

1.3 Popular culture 'fictional' constructions of LGBTQ+ parents

Beyond news media, there are also increasing visibilities of LGBTQ+ parents in popular culture globally. This includes in-print books, movies, television serials, reality TV/ documentaries, and video gaming. It is where depictions of LGBTQ+ parents are mainstreamed or exposed to young people that these parents become considered *most controversial*, and the concept of 'inappropriately exposing youth to sexual things' is still a false flag waved against the dangers of even quite tame LGBTQ+ parents depictions. In the early 2000s in Australia for example, a lesbian couple was depicted visually in a television clip taking their daughter to a fun-park on the early childhood show 'Play School' for the first time, to great political and media backlash (Cubby, 2004; Nguyen, 2015). The acting Prime Minister, John Anderson, and senior Government ministers lashed out at the ABC for 'exposing young children' to same-sex parenting. The Communications Minister, Daryl Williams, called the ABC managing director, Russell Balding, to 'express his concern' that the program had aired the segment – asking him to pass the complaint to the ABC board (Cubby, 2004; Nguyen, 2015). Over a decade later, the launch of the documentary film *Gayby Baby* into school environments as a resource interviewing LGBTQ+ parents' children, still garnered some extremely negative press (Tomazin, 2016).

Empirical evidence from examinations of popular media representations of LGBTQ+ parents highlights accounts that are often either wholly bent towards normalising or pathologising them (Riggs, 2011). Damien Riggs explored five filmic portrayals of gay men variously engaged in fostering and adoptive arrangements between 2000 and 2007: *Cachorro (Bear Cub), The Conrad Boys, Holiday Heart, Get Your Stuff,* and *Shelter*. Representing both biological and nonbiological relations, these texts displayed four dominant themes: (1) capacities of gay men to parent under various circumstances; (2) relationships between gay men's sexual and parenting identities; (3) the agency of children cared for by gay men; and (4) constructions of kinship. There is the possibility of the 'romantic' gay parent in such mainstream cultural representations. Romance also emerges in other TV series characters including: *Soap's* (1977) Jodie; *The Tracey Ullman Show* (1982) Dave and William; *ER's* (1994) Kerry and Sandy; and *Friends* (1995) Carol and Susan; though largely in peripheral themes. Successful and stable provider roles for LGBT parents were further emphasised in direct central characters since the 2000s, including: *Queer as Folk's* (2000) Melanie and Lindsay; *Modern Family's* Cameron and Mitchell; *Greys Anatomy's* Callie and Arizona; *Six Feet Under's* (2003) Fisher and Charles; *The Wire's* (2005) Kima and Cheryl; *Will and Grace's* (1998) Joe and Larry; *The New Normal's* (2012) David and Bryan and *The Fosters'*(2013) Stef and Lena. Regardless of the genre such constructions emphasised mostly sanitised, de-sexualised acceptability politics emphasising parents' roles as hard-working professionals in mostly long-term relationships and considering challenges in their family constellations.

Depictions shift dramatically in the limited, largely 'indie' genre media created for consumption by LGBTQ+ communities themselves. It is mainly here the LGBTQ+ parent or their offspring is portrayed without being sanitised of sexuality or complexity, and still affirmed. For example, Patricia Highsmith's 1952 novel 'The Price of Salt' provided an early positive construction of a lesbian mother (Carol) when doing so was contentious; she had to use a pseudonym

(Claire Morgan) without the support of her usual publisher, in a move considered career suicide. Whilst the book since became iconic after being turned into the 2015 film *Carol*, it was initially considered 'pulp fiction' for its depiction of a lesbian divorcee losing custody of her daughter Rindy for her love for partner Therese. The book shows Carol ultimately trying to balance her sexual, romantic and parental roles... a then unpublishable phenomenon. The casual indie computer game/ phone dating simulator app *Dream Daddy* released via Steam in 2017 allows the player similarly to both inhabit a Dad character whose goal is 'to meet and romance other hot Dads' and to maintain a good parenting relationship with their child character, its description on Steam reading:

> You and your daughter have just moved into the sleepy seaside town of Maple Bay only to discover that everyone in your neighborhood is a single, dateable Dad! Will you go out with Teacher Dad? Goth Dad? Bad Dad? Or any of the other cool Dads...

The depiction offers a vision of solo fatherhood and an active if complex dating life (potentially with transgender, genderqueer and gay dads of various cultural and social class backgrounds) with highs and lows, without requiring compromising in favour of either one's parenting or LGBTQ+ identities. However, the ideal or 'winning' scenarios across most indie depictions still valorise queer coupledom.

Depictions with lead transgender parents emerged more strongly, recently. These included the 2005 drama-comedy *Transamerica* about a trans woman meeting up with a son she didn't know she'd had, the 2013 indie film *52 Tuesdays* showing a transgender father and his daughter navigating their relationship and the 2014–2019 *Transparent* drama-comedy web series about a trans woman coming out to her self-absorbed children. In all films a complex sexual liberation theme is expressed through the offspring; the parents themselves are largely grappling with their gender identity and shifting parenting role – whether as a divorcee or solo parents. *Orange is the New Black* (2013) is a television series featuring transgender parent Sophia, notably played by an African American transgender woman where mostly transgender parents are depicted by white cisgender actors. She notably has storylines exploring her sexual relationship with her wife as a transgender woman where most transgender parent characters are not afforded active sex lives – though the relationship becomes platonic. Overall, the strong themes of financial and relationship stability emphasised in the 'positive' constructions of LGB parents in popular culture; and more solitary depictions of transgender parenting; may (like media depictions) leave education stakeholders with stereotyped ideas. These may impact LGBTQ+ parents' anticipated and actual treatment within school environments and promote certain norms for their acceptability that should be re-considered in policy.

1.4 What's policy got to do with It?

International legal frameworks including the *Universal Declaration of Human Rights* (United Nations/UN, 1948), *International Covenant on Economic, Social and Cultural Rights* (UN, 1996), the *UN Convention on the Rights of the Child* (UN, 1989), and *Sustainable Development Goals* (United Nations, 2015) view safe and inclusive learning environments as a basic human right. These legal frameworks include mandating primary or elementary education as compulsory and strongly encouraging or mandating secondary education for youth (UN, 1989). Consequently, parents are similarly mandated to engage with their child's educational environments, managing their schooling progressions. Countries approach the human right to education and protections offered to LGBTQ+ parents variably depending on their legal, social and cultural contexts.

Although more countries around the world are legalising same-sex marriage (30 to date; Masci & Desilver, 2019), few support LGBTQ+ parents. Around 67 countries and jurisdictions cast consensual same-sex behaviours and relationships as illegal with severe potential punishments including imprisonment or death penalties (Botha et al., 2020). Other countries exclude specific mention of LGBTQ+ individuals, couple or parents in legislation and subsequent treatment may be determined by the social, cultural or judiciary mores (Botha et al., 2020). Other countries include specific protections for LGBTQ+ couples, and parents in employment, education, freedom from discrimination/hate crimes, recognition of same-sex partnerships and legal rights to adoption (Botha et al., 2020). National protections for LGBTQ+ parents including marriage equality, recognition of same-sex defacto relationships, same-sex parents' access to joint adoption and legal rights to adopt same-sex partners children are highlighted in Table 1.1. Whilst laws and policies internationally are constantly evolving – and occasionally rescinded after being advanced or ignored in practice – the table reveals overall *trends*. Europe and the Americas, which are more strongly impacted by regional networking through rights-based polity and health networks, have many more protections in place impacting

LGBTQ+ parents – with notable exceptions like Russia where 'LGBT Propaganda' bans in schools can make LGBTQ+ parents' visibility dangerous. Conversely, Africa, Asia and Oceania will need many more global and contextually specific coordinated efforts linking into and supporting local movements for LGBTQ+ parents' positions to advance – with notable exceptions for countries which could be leading local collaborative change efforts like Australia, New Zealand, South Africa, Israel, Japan and Taiwan.

Legal protection of LGBTQ+ couples and parents may coincide with greater equality in other aspects of life, and Table 1.1 does show that there are some anti-discrimination protections for sexual orientation in all of these contexts, and gender affirmation in most. These protections usually pre-existed and are a contributing factor if not a pre-condition for the coupling and parenting protections, though not always causal (Jones, 2019). However, countries and jurisdictions can also include cultural norms, societal views and other laws that can limit the freedoms of LGBTQ+ parents compared to heterosexual or cis-gendered individuals (Botha et al., 2020). For example, Australia legalised same-sex marriage in 2017 and offers legal protection from discrimination for LGBTQ+ people in education and employment (NSW Parliamentary Counsel, 1977). However, these protections vary depending on the state an individual resides in and may not apply in religious schools (NSW Parliamentary Counsel, 1977). Additionally, the methods of achieving marriage equality for same-sex parents have differed around the world, with some countries requiring votes or surveys while others solely used judiciary and government processes (Botha et al., 2020). In 2017 most Australians indicated support for marriage equality laws (or same-sex marriage), suggesting increased acceptance in the general society of LGBTQ+ diversity potentially including coupling and parenting (Australian Bureau of Statistics/ABS, 2017).

National and state educational policies can also differ to the extent they include parents in schools. In some countries, such as Australia, there is an emphasis on the need for schools to include the diversity of students and their families within school policies, procedures and practices. However, the types of diversity explicitly included differ, as highlighted in Table 1.2. Generally, these policies state:

- schools need to build collaborative respectful relationships with parents,
- schools should continually review and adapt teacher training, policies and practices to meet parents and students' needs,

Table 1.1 International Legal Recognition of LGBTQ+ Parents by Region and Nation

Country/ Territory	Marriage Equality or Same-Sex Marriage	Protections Sexual Orientation (×), Gender Affirmation (Ga).	Recognition of Same-Sex Partnership Civil Unions	Same-Sex Parent Joint Adoption	Second Parent Adoption by Same-Sex Couples
Africa					
South Africa	×	×/Ga	×	×	×
Latin America and the Caribbean					
Argentina	×	×/Ga	×	×	×
Brazil	×	×/Ga	×	×	×
Chile		×/Ga	×		
Colombia	×	×/Ga	×	×	×
Costa Rica	×	×/Ga		×	×
Ecuador	×	×/Ga	×		
Mexico	×	×/Ga	Limited	Limited	Limited
Uruguay	×	×/Ga	×	×	×
North America					
Canada	×	×/Ga	×	×	×
United States	×	×/Ga Limited	Limited	×	×
Asia					
Israel		×/Ga	×	×	×
Japan		×/Ga	Limited		
Taiwan	×	×/Ga	×		×
Europe					
Andorra		×	×	×	×
Austria	×	×	×	×	×
Belgium	×	×/Ga	×	×	×
Croatia		×/Ga	×		
Cyprus		×/Ga	×		
Czech Republic		×/Ga	×		
Denmark	×	×/Ga		×	×
Estonia		×/Ga	×		×
Finland	×	×/Ga		×	×
France	×	×/Ga	×	×	×
Germany	×	×/Ga		×	×

(*Continued*)

Country/ Territory	Marriage Equality or Same-Sex Marriage	Protections Sexual Orientation (×), Gender Affirmation (Ga).	Recognition of Same-Sex Partnership Civil Unions	Same-Sex Parent Joint Adoption	Second Parent Adoption by Same-Sex Couples
Greece		×/Ga	×		
Hungary		×/Ga	×		
Iceland	×	×/Ga		×	×
Italy		×/Ga	×		
Liechtenstein		×	×		
Luxembourg	×	×/Ga	×	×	×
Malta	×	×/Ga	×	×	×
Monaco		×	×		
Montenegro		×/Ga	×		
Netherlands	×	×/Ga	×	×	×
Norway	×	×/Ga		×	×
Portugal	×	×/Ga	×	×	×
San Marino		×	×		×
Slovenia		×	×		×
Spain	×	×/Ga	×	×	×
Sweden	×	×/Ga		×	×
Switzerland		×/Ga	×		×
United Kingdom	×	×/Ga	×	×	×
Oceania					
Australia	×	×/Ga	×	×	×
New Zealand	×	×/Ga	×	×	×

Botha et al.(2020, pp. 325–330); Jones (2019, pp. 87–112).

- schools must adopt inclusive teaching practices and lessons to include and represent the school community's diversity, and
- amendments to school practices should be based on evidence.

However, these policies more commonly include more mainstream forms of family diversity such as multi-culturalism/-lingualism and religion rather than LGBTQ+ diversity; only two states (Western Australia and Tasmania) explicitly mention strategies inclusive of LGBTQ+ parented families.

Additionally, the policies commonly place the responsibility on individual schools and educators to create welcoming school contexts for parents through activities like teacher training and inclusive practices, dependent on the diversity included in school communities and classrooms. That is, LGBTQ+ parents need to be 'out' and present within school environments for schools and teachers to take the next steps

Table 1.2 Australian National and State Educational Policies Inclusive of Families

Level	Policy/Source	Policy Topics	Suggested Strategies
National	Melbourne Declaration on Educational Goals for Young Australians (Ministerial Council on Employment, Training and Young Affairs (MCEETYA), 2008).	• Understanding and respect for social, cultural, and religious diversity. • Provide school environments free of discrimination based on sexual orientation and gender. • School's collaborative with family and local community to develop inclusive practices.	• Professional development for school staff. • Partnerships between families, students, and the broader community. • School environments improved with evidence-based data to inform policy, resources, family-school relationships, and teacher practices.
	Australian Professional Standards for Teaching (Australian Institute for Teaching and School Leadership Limited, 2011).	• Developed from Melbourne Declaration. • Focus on professional guidelines to be met by current Australian teachers. • Create and maintain supportive learning environments; engage in professional learning and engage professionally with families and the community.	• Teachers know diverse cultural backgrounds and social characteristics of students and are accommodated within classroom activities (1.1). • Teachers adapt teaching strategies/ processes to meet the needs of students (1.3). • Inclusive school activities and communications (3.5). • Ongoing assessment, reflection, and adaptation to teaching practices, school procedures and professional development (3.6, 4.4, 6.2, 7.2). • Teachers build professional relationships with families and contextualise teaching practices (3.7, 7.3).

(Continued)

Level	Policy/Source	Policy Topics	Suggested Strategies
	Australian Curriculum and Assessment Reporting Authority (ACARA, 2019).	• Developed from Melbourne Declaration. • Focus on students with disability, gifted and talented students and English as an Additional Language or Dialect (EALD). • Provision of services and resources available differ by state.	• EALD directions: Inclusive curriculum in consideration of culture and linguistics. • Ensure teaching practices and procedures consider additional or alternative understandings to family relationships, utilise student's cultural understandings and build shared knowledge. Including: resources that reflect cultures, different perspectives in classrooms; personalise learning by drawing on family/cultural background or histories; professional development in cultural/linguistic diversity and inclusive practices in schools.
	Family-School Partnerships: A Guide for Schools and Families (Department of Education, Employment and Workplace Relations, 2019).	• Building collaborative Family-school relationships. • Engage families in school processes and procedures. • Respect and understand family diversity in school community.	• Collaborative effort of family and school to improve processes, practices, and policies. • Inclusive teaching practices. • Professional training of school staff. • Policies/documents that explicitly outline focus on school-family relationship strategies.
Australian Capital Territory (ACT)	Strategic Plan 2018–2021: A Leading Learning Organisation (ACT Government, 2019).	• Embrace diversity and collaborative partnerships. • Personalised and flexible pedagogy for each student. • Ongoing school system improvements and focus on engaging parents in schools. • Evidence based practice.	• Professional development in staff. • Sourcing and utilising feedback from families to improve policy, procedures, resources, and teaching practices.

New South Wales (NSW)	School Excellence Framework (NSW Government, 2017).	• Guidelines on best practice school procedures and practices. • Teachers engage with students and families collaboratively to meet the needs of students and families in schools respective of diversity. • Evidence-based practice and ongoing improvements.	• Collaborative development of school policies, procedures &practices with families. • Inclusive differentiated curriculum, practices, and policies to accommodate students and families.
Northern Territory (NT)	Framework for Inclusion 2019–2029 (NT Government, 2019).	• School system improvements for students, families/communities, and school staff. • Focus on disabilities, behavioural difficulties, identified vulnerable students. • Inclusive education with focus on differentiated support, community engagement. • Continual improvement to practices/professional development of staff to meet student needs. • Collaboration with parents/external services for system improvements. • Evidence-based practice.	• Inclusive curriculum, policies, practices to meet individual student needs. • Collaboration with parents/community in improving school systems. • Meet the holistic needs of students and families. • Professional development on inclusivity.
Queensland (QLD)	Advancing Partnerships – Parent and Community Engagement Framework (Queensland Government, 2019).	• Guidelines to improve collaborative respectful relationships between schools and families. • Respect and understanding of cultural differences in families and accommodations of diversity in school systems.	• Collaborative design and implementation of school-wide inclusivity in practices, policies, procedures, and teaching approaches. • Professional development in school staff.

(Continued)

Level	Policy/Source	Policy Topics	Suggested Strategies
South Australia (SA)	Wellbeing for Learning and Life: A Framework for Building Resilience and Wellbeing in Children and Young People (Department of Education and Child Development, 2016).	• Build collaborative and respectful relationships with schools and families. • Inclusive practices that value diversity including gender identity and sexuality. • Evidence based practice.	• Engaging with school community members including students and families to build inclusive welcoming environments.
Tasmania	Guidelines for Supporting Sexual and Gender Diversities in Schools and Colleges (Tasmanian Department of Education, 2012).	• Creating a safe school community environment for LGBT students, teachers, and families. • School community members uphold acceptance and understanding of LGBT being another form of 'normal' diversity. • Evidence-based proactive approach/ response.	• Explicit mention of LGBT school community members in the policy. • Inclusive/gender-neutral language. • Inclusive curriculum, policy, professional development for staff, physical representation (posters/books), resources and materials.
Victoria	Framework for Improving Student Outcomes (Department of Education Victoria, 2019).	• Active engagement with parents and carers to improve school policy, procedures, and practice. • Evidence-based approach with the ongoing review.	• Ensure school policies, practices, procedures, and curriculum are inclusive of family diversity.

| *Western Australia (WA)* | Guidelines for supporting sexual and gender diversity in schools (Equal Opportunity Commission of Western Australia, 2013). | • Focus on safe learning environments, discrimination, and bullying.
• Inclusivity of LGBT students and family diversity as a reflection of normal form of diversity.
• School to accept and understand all forms of diversity in schools.
• Evidence-based proactive/responsive school-wide approach. | • Inclusive policies, plans, language, and curriculum that promote positive school culture.
• Provision of supportive networks in schools.
• Explicit school commitment to inclusive schools reflected in communications to all school community members.
• Gender-neutral language in school communications.
• Professional development for staff on LGBT topics/issues.
• Collaborative work between parents and schools to develop supports in schools.
• Provision of resources/materials to support LGBT students e.g., posters/books. |

(such as training) in building collaborative relationships. This can prove difficult: not all parents disclose their sexual orientation or gender identity to their child's schools. Further, both parents and teachers have been found to fear potential backlash from school communities (e.g. leadership, other parents, students and locals) when representing and discussing LGBTQ+ topics in schools (Lindsay et al., 2006).

The erratic progress in LGBTQ+ rights recognition broadly by UN, UNESCO, and Australian national and state laws as well as in different education sectors' policies and in different schools, may affect certainty for Australian LGBTQ+ parents around their protection and safety in education contexts. Further, existing protections are often under threat. Recently a stream of national and state-specific attempts at creating an allowance for anti-LGBTQ+ discrimination through the drafting of bills using religious freedom to justify bigotry enables the breaking of existing laws; the expulsion and mistreatment of LGBTQ+ people from education contexts or the banning of educational efforts to acknowledge and include them (Australian Government, 2019). School leadership and educators may further be hesitant given the considerable media, policy, political and public debate dedicated to 'if and how' LGBTQ+ parents should be acknowledged, represented and included within mainstream school systems (Law, 2017).

1.5 A research & policy gap?

There is an evident need for social organisations to investigate, develop and implement inclusive policies, procedures, and practices to reflect the new legal equality offered to LGBTQ+ parents and their families. However, such progressions in policy are often hindered by the highly politicised and polarised views of the inclusion of LGBTQ+ identities within school systems, the relative lack of research on LGBTQ+ parents' experiences in school contexts, and little incorporation of LGBTQ+ parents views on 'if and how' they should be included in heated school policy debates... which exist against the backdrop of problematic and influential media and popular culture constructions of LGBTQ+ parents described in this chapter.

To date, research has explored teachers' perspectives on LGBTQ+ related supports in schools, LGBTQ+ parent experiences within school contexts, and offered school guides for LGBTQ+ inclusive school practices (Cloughessy et al., 2019; Goldberg & Smith, 2014; UNESCO, 2016). However little research considers 'LGBTQ+ parents' views around how they would like to be systematically included and represented within school contexts. Yet, international research studies exploring LGBTQ+ parent navigations in school contexts highlight several unique challenges and potential supports that could inform potential proactive and inclusive school policies, procedures, and practices (Cloughessy et al., 2019; Goldberg & Smith, 2014). Positive relationships between parents and teachers is related to several beneficial outcomes for students including prosocial behaviour, academic achievement and higher education attainment (Henderson & Mapp, 2002). Teaching professional standards and educational policy recognise the benefits of quality parent-school relationships and stress the need for schools to build collaborative relationships between parents, teachers and schools as a method to accommodate diversity (AITSL, 2011). Notably, these education policies often fail to explicitly mention LGBTQ+ parents or families as a possible form of family diversity. As a result, parents may face school contexts that are under-prepared to accommodate, include or represent them (Cloughessy et al., 2019; Fox, 2007).

1.6 The aims of this book

In recognition of the potential lack of policy regarding LGBTQ+ groups in education, the United Nations (UNESCO, 2016) and educational authorities (AITSL, 2011) stress the need for policy development to be informed by previous research and the views of the minority group they serve. This is to ensure that policy development:

- acknowledges potential changes in cultural or social views toward minority groups,
- adopts a 'holistic' lens in exploring a range of potential challenging experiences and supportive strategies to identify unmet needs of minority groups, and
- recognises the potential for school contexts to be supportive organisations for the health and well-being of school community members (AITSL, 2011; UNESCO, 2016).

However, research studies exploring different aspects of LGBTQ+ parents and their experiences in social contexts have been conducted within a wide range of disciplines (such as psychology, health and sociology) and by a breadth of interested parties (e.g. LGBTQ+ not-for-profit organisations and research institutes), which aren't commonly included within the discussion of LGBTQ+ parent and school research. In keeping with the recommendations of policy development guidelines, this book accordingly aims to explore previous research on LGBTQ+ parents, identify unmet needs and account for differences in cultural or social views toward LGBTQ+ minority groups. The research questions developed for this study include:

1 How has research exploring LGBTQ+ parents changed over time?
2 What are some of the challenges or supports experienced by LGBTQ+ parents in Australia that may be useful in informing future educational policy reforms?
3 What are the views of LGBTQ+ parents on 'if and how' they would like to be included in their child's school context?
4 What are LGBTQ+ parents' valued experiences in school environments and their suggestions for improvements in schools?
5 How can schools, educators, policy makers and educational authorities create more welcoming school contexts for LGBTQ+ parents, from the perspective of LGBTQ+ parents' themselves?

1.7 Summary of key points

The key points that can be summarised for this chapter include:

• Media and popular culture may be points of reference on LGBTQ+ parents for many education stakeholders.
• Both the dominant negative and positive constructions of the group offered by media and popular culture sources include partial, flawed and problematic ideas which LGBTQ+ parents then must battle against in education spaces/thinking.
• There has been significant debate internationally, but little research foregrounds LGBTQ+ parents, on 'if and how' LGBTQ+ parents should be included in schools.
• National policies and laws, and education policies, differ in their treatment and explicit mention of LGBTQ+ individuals, couples and parents.
• 'Good' policy development should include a review of previous research to identify potential challenges and unmet needs, and views from the minority groups served.

1.8 Conclusion & next chapters

This chapter highlighted the need for this publication in informing LGBTQ+ related inclusive school supports, given the problematic representation of LGBTQ+ parents in media and popular culture and the uneven progression alignment between LGBTQ+ rights and education policy. Chapter two reviews research exploring LGBTQ+ parented families. Chapter three introduces a social-psychological framework.

Chapter four discusses the Australian focal study of LGBTQ+ parents and schools at the core of the book; including parents' characteristics and school environments. Chapter five highlights parents' perspectives and justifications for LGBTQ+ related school supports. Chapter six discusses parents' positive experiences in schools and recommendations for creating more welcoming school contexts, and Chapter seven provides over-arching key findings and a list of inclusion strategies endorsed for different education stakeholders.

References

ABS. (2017). *1800.0- Australian Marriage Law Postal Survey, 2017.* Retrieved from https://www.abs.gov.au/websitedbs/D3310114.nsf/home/AMLPS+-+Privacy+Policy

ACARA. (2019). *Student Diversity.* Retrieved from https://www.acara.edu.au/curriculum/student-diversity.

ACT Government. (2019). *Strategic Plan 2018–21.* Canberra: ACT Education Directorate.

AITSL. (2011). *Australian Professional Standards for Teachers.* Melbourne: Education Council.

Australian Government. (2019). *Draft Religious Freedom Bills Package.* Retrieved from https://www.ag.gov.au/Consultations/Pages/religious-freedom-bills.aspx

Botha, K., Lelis, R., López De La Peña, E., & Tan, D. (2020). *State-Sponsored Homophobia.* Geneva: ILGA.

Carlile, A., & Paechter, C. (2018). *LGBTQI Parented Families and Schools.* London: Routledge.

Cloughessy, K., Waniganayake, M., & Blatterer, H. (2019). The good and the bad. *Journal of Research in Childhood Education,33*(3),446–458.

Cubby, B. (2004). Play School's lesbian tale sparks outrage. *Sydney Morning Herald.* Retrieved from https://www.smh.com.au/national/play-schools-lesbian-tale-sparks-outrage-20040604-gdj23z.html

Department for Education and Child Development. (2016). *Wellbeing for Learning and Life.* Adelaide: SA Government.

Department of Education, Employment and Workplace Relations. (2019). *Family-School Partnerships Framework.* Canberra: Australian Government.

Department of Education Victoria. (2019). *Framework for Improving Student Outcomes.* Melbourne: Victorian Government.

Equal Opportunity Commission of Western Australia. (2013). *Guidelines for Supporting Sexual and Gender Diversity in Schools: Sexuality Discrimination & Homophobic Bullying.* Perth: WA Equal Opportunity Commission.

Fox, R. K. (2007). One of the hidden diversities in schools. *Childhood Education, 83*(5), 277–281.

Goldberg, A. E., & Smith, J. Z. (2014). Preschool selection considerations and experiences of school mistreatment among lesbian, gay, and heterosexual adoptive parents. *Early Childhood Research Quarterly, 29*(1), 64–75.

Henderson, A., & Mapp, K. (2002). *A New Wave of Evidence*. Austin: South-west Educational Development Laboratory.

Hook, G. (2017). The child's best interests? In T. Jones (Ed.), *Bent Street* (Vol 2). Melbourne: Clouds of Magellan. pp.26–33.

Jones, T. (2019). Chapter 5. Legal landscapes. In T. Jones, L. Coll, L. van Leent &Y. Taylor (Eds.), *Uplifting Gender and Sexuality Education Research* (pp. 87–112). Palgrave Macmillan: Basingstoke.

Kahn, H. (2014). *LGBT Parents on American Television*. Hattiesburg: University of Southern Missisippi.

Law, B. (2017). Moral panic 101. *Quarterly Essay,67*, 1–80.

Lindsay, J., Perlesz, A., Brown, R., McNair, R., De Vaus, D., & Pitts, M. (2006). Stigma or respect. *Sociology,40*(6),1059–1077.

Lynch, I., & Morison, T. (2016*)*. Gay men as parents. *Feminism & Psychology,26*, 188–206.

Masci, D., & Desilver, D. (2019). *A Global Snapshot of Same-Sex Marriage*. Washington: Pew.

MCEETYA. (2008). *Melbourne Declaration on Educational Goals for Young Australians*. Melbourne: MCEETYA.

Nguyen, T. H. L. (2015). New Zealand same-sex marriage legislation in the Australian media. *Journal of Media & Cultural Studies, 29*(3), 287–303.

NSW Government. (2017). *School Excellence Framework*. Sydney: NSW Government.

NSW Parliamentary Counsel. (1997). *Anti-Discrimination Act 1997*. 48 Cong. Rec.

NT Government. (2019). *Framework for Inclusion 2019–29*. Darwin: NT Government.

Queensland Government. (2019). *Advancing Partnerships*. Brisbane: QLD Government.

Riggs, D. (2011). 'Let's go to the movies'. *Journal of GLBT Family Studies, 7*(3), 297–312.

Tasmanian Department of Education. (2012). *Guidelines for Supporting Sexual and Gender Diversity in Schools and Colleges*. Hobart: Tasmanian Government.

Tomazin, F. (2016). Gayby Baby. *The Age*. Retrieved from http://www.theage.com.au/victoria/gayby-baby-schools-to-get-a-lesson-in-family-diversity-20160507-goouoe.html

UN. (1948). *The Universal Declaration of Human Rights*. Paris: UN.

UN. (1989). *Conventions on the Rights of the Child*. New York: UN.

UN. (1996). *International Convenant on Economic, Social and Cultural Rights Article 27 Resolution 2200A (XXI)*. Geneva: UN.

UN. (2015) *The Sustainable Developmen Goals*. Paris: UN.

UNESCO. (2016). *Out in the Open*. Paris: UNESCO.

Von Doussa, H., & Power, J. (2019). A lesson in queer. In T. Jones (Ed.), *Bent Street* (Vol. 2, pp. 55–67). Melbourne: Clouds of Magellan.

2 Reviewing LGBTQ+ parent research in & beyond schools

LGBTQ+ parents reflect on: the literature (Un)available
Too many people live sheltered lives, they are not against lgbt (parents) but are not even aware we exist, it would be nice to see some recognition.

(Amber, 43 yrs, South Australia)

I think young people access this info online but there is a lot of negative and misleading content that is unregulated. Young people need access to the right information within mainstream settings such as schools.

(Harper, 57 yrs, Victoria)

There is no education on the matter in their schools.

(Josephine, 43 yrs, South Australia)

At the moment our children's peers are getting information from their homes only about same sex families and this is not always positive. Our children are having to address that themselves, which can lead to a feeling of isolation in the school yard. It is also important for our children to see families similar to their own represented in school learning materials.

(Madelyn, 42 yrs, New South Wales)

2.1 Introduction: the LGBTQ+ parent literature

The literature on LGBTQ+ parents is growing and changing over time. These changes are affected by shifts in social, legal, and medical views of LGBTQ+ identities. Early research on LGBTQ+ identities in the 1960s and 1970s tended to emerge from research based in the US and UK that adopted medicalised or 'traditional' psychological

DOI: 10.4324/9781003167471-2

lenses (e.g. Bene, 1965). This research developed in contexts that assumed that gender identities/expressions and sexual orientations that were not exclusively heterosexual or cis-gendered were illegal, socially taboo, a potential risk to society, and considered disorders of the mind (Bene, 1965; Bieber, 1962).

Later research from the 1980s and 1990s shifted to studies adopting sociological theoretical frameworks applying Butler's, Foucault's and Feminist post-structuralist thinking with a focus on exploring how parents formed families, organised home life, and functioned in social contexts such as schools (McNair et al., 2002; van Dam, 2004). These research trends and limitations inform educational stakeholders, researchers, policy makers and educational professionals – including their misconceptions, negative assumptions, and knowledge gaps on LGBTQ+ family diversity (Casper et al., 1992; Herbstrith et al., 2013; Robinson, 2002).

This chapter explores the key framings, timelines, researchers, themes, and limitations four key bodies of LGBTQ+ literature (see Table 2.1): Anti-LGBTQ+ studies since the 1950s+; LGBTQ+ parent and child development studies emerging since the 1970s+; LGBTQ+ family diversity and family functioning studies emerging since the 1990s+; and LGBTQ+ parents and school studies merging since the 1990s+ and 2000s+. It concludes by noting key findings and research gaps.

2.2 Anti-LGBTQ+ studies (individuals and parents)

2.2.1 *Anti-LGBTQ+ research pre-1990s*

Traditional psychological methods of exploring LGBTQ+ individuals and their parents were first evident in the 1960s–1970s (e.g. Bieber, 1962). At the time, this type of research commonly developed in social, cultural, medical, psychological, legal and judicial environments. These contexts viewed LGBTQ+ identities as largely illegal, immoral, an illness or disease, and a potential risk to society (Drescher, 2015; Gonsiorek, 1982a). Re-affirming these ideas of LGBTQ+ identities being an illness of the mind, homosexuality was listed as a diagnosable disorder in the first and second edition of the *Diagnostic and Statistical Manual of Mental Disorders* spanning from 1952 to 1974 (1st edition; DSM-I; American Psychiatric Association/APA, 1952; 2nd edition; DSM-II; APA, 1968). As a result of the medicalised and pathologizing views of homosexuality and other LBTQ+ identities including the later use of gender identity disorder and then dysphoria for transgender individuals (Drescher & Byne, 2012), researchers and practitioners

Table 2.1 Dominant Conceptual Framings of LGBTQ+ Parent Research

	Anti – LGBTQ+ Studies	LGBTQ+ Parent and Child Development Studies	LGBTQ+ Parented Family Diversity and Family Functioning Studies	LGBTQ+ Parents in School Contexts Studies
Dominance:	1960s–1990s	1980s–2000s	1990s+	1990s+
Key Researchers:	Bene (1965), Cameron and Cameron (1996), Snortum et al. (1969).	Anderssen et al. (2002), Golombok et al. (2013); Stacey and Biblarz (2001), Tasker (2005).	Dempsey (2010, 2013), Eliason (1996), Gahan (2018), McNair et al. (2008), Perlesz et al. (2006), Power et al. (2010), van Dam (2004).	Cloughessy and Waniganayake (2015), Eliason (1996), Goldberg et al. (2014), Hegde et al. (2014), Kosciw and Diaz (2008), Robinson (2002).
Themes:	-Medical view of LGBTQ+ individuals and families. -Focus on aetiology of mental health disorders. -Gender norms/ parenting traits of parents of homosexuals.	-Developed to inform legal practitioners and courts in custody battles. -Comparative studies of child development in heterosexual/ homosexual parented children. -Sets heterosexual parents as Gold-Star in childhood development.	-LGBTQ+ parented family diversity demographics including: • Roles/configurations of parental figures; • Pathways to conception; • Peer/familial relationships; • Education; • Income; & • Employment.	-Barriers/Stressors: • Exclusion, discrimination and stigmatising experiences; • Teachers - attitudes, religious values, professional concerns; • Peers – both student and parent beliefs/values and reactions to LGBTQ+ parented families; & • School administration – religious beliefs, recognition of diverse family structures.

(Continued)

	Anti – LGBTQ+ Studies	*LGBTQ+ Parent and Child Development Studies*	*LGBTQ+ Parented Family Diversity and Family Functioning Studies*	*LGBTQ+ Parents in School Contexts Studies*
Dominance:	*1960s–1990s*	*1980s–2000s*	*1990s+*	*1990s+*
	-Anecdotal evidence of risks of non-traditional forms of the family including: • Sexual orientation transmission; • Developing Psychopathologies; & • Maladjusted child development.	- No statistically significant difference was found in: • Gender roles; • Pro-social behaviour; • Cognitive development; & • Psycho-sexual development.	-Family functioning in different contexts: • Supportive peers/ familial ties; • Stigma, exclusion and discrimination from service providers; & • Schools and health care are particularly stressful contexts.	-Recommendations: • Policy; • Explicit inclusion of diverse families in brochures/websites/ documents • Teacher and administrative staff training/education; • Inclusion of diverse families in the curriculum; • Inclusion of artefacts that reflect family diversity in classrooms; • Diverse families accommodated in forms/paperwork; & • Collaborative relationships between families and schools to develop inclusive school communities and welcoming environments.

within this school of thought sought to identify factors that contributed to the development of a homosexuality diagnosis, potential methods to treat 'the troubled homosexual' or gendered 'invert', and gain further insight into the characteristics of individuals receiving a diagnosis. Although not specifically targeting LGBTQ+ parents, one branch of this research attempted to explore the potential for the quality and characteristics of parent-child relationships to be a contributing factor to the development of homosexuality in individuals (Bene, 1965; Bieber, 1962; Evans, 1969; Snortum et al., 1969).

This body of research was heavily influenced by the Freudian theory of psycho-sexual development in children (Drescher, 2015). It placed a strong emphasis on exploring socially and culturally acceptable gender roles and behaviours exhibited by parents and children (Bene, 1965; Bieber, 1962). The general aim of this type of research was to identify potential family characteristics and parent-child relationships that could explain the 'abnormal development' of homosexual identities in individuals, and subsequently inform clinical practice and potential treatment (Drescher, 2015). Gender roles and behaviours in parents typically explored in these studies included traditionally 'masculine' traits in fathers such as competitive sports and stoicism and traditionally 'feminine' traits in mothers such as being nurturing and caregivers (Bieber, 1962). As a result of the social, cultural, and patriarchal biases and norms embedded within this research area, researchers tended to argue that homosexuality and gender inversion (and other mental disorders) developed within family environments that failed to uphold 'traditional' gender norms and appropriate role-modelling. Examples of the conclusions drawn from this research included non-heterosexual identities and mental disorders developed from weak, absent, ineffectual, or poor relationships with father figures and mothers who were seductive, over-indulgent, over-attached and attempted to 'feminise' their sons (Bene, 1965; Snortum et al., 1969). The re-occurring argument that LGBTQ+ identities developed as a result of family characteristics that failed to consist of socially and culturally accepted gender norms – such as the 'masculine' father, and the 'feminine' mother – was a pervasive argument that continued to be influential in legislative contexts during the 1970s and 1980s (Beargie, 1988). However, more contemporary researchers have highlighted various limitations evident within this type of research including methodological flaws and researcher bias (Drescher, 2015; Gonsiorek, 1982a).

Researchers such as Gonsiorek (1982a, 1982b) and Drescher (2015) have reviewed this body of literature and found it to contain various challenges and limitations. These particularly include problems in relation to the definition and categorisation of homosexuality, the limited scope of the research methodologies, over-generalised arguments drawn from results and the heavy influence of social, historical, cultural and medicalised, biased views of homosexuality (Gonsiorek, 1982a).

Sampling bias was strongly evident in these studies with participants being drawn from identified or suspected homosexuals (particularly gay males) in 'non-typical' settings such as clinical institutions, prisons and military service. Such sampling limited the generalisability of findings to LGBTQ+ populations outside of these environments (Gonsiorek, 1982a). Further critiques of the DSM and LGBTQ+ individual-parent research at the time included the potential bias of cultural and societal gender norms – where individuals and parents who did not adhere to 'acceptable' gendered behaviours in countries such as the UK, USA and Australia were deemed a potential risk for maladjusted child development (Gonsiorek, 1982b). Additionally, these studies failed to include research that explored LGBTQ+ parents specifically. Yet, such sentiments about the potential for parents that fail to uphold traditional family structures and socially acceptable gender norms are still relevant today. They have been associated with less positive attitudes toward LGBTQ+ forms of family diversity, opposition to LGBTQ+ inclusive curriculums in school contexts and educational professionals' stereotypical beliefs about 'normal' child development characteristics (Casper et al., 1992).

2.2.2 *Anti-LGBTQ+ research 1990s+*

Since the 1990s research literature has seen a re-emergence of anti-LGBTQ+ parent papers including what appear to be peer-reviewed articles and grey literature (non-peer-reviewed publications). These publications are often authored by known affiliates to conservative religious organisations. They may be seen as a response to increasing trends of greater representation, recognition and acknowledgement of LGBTQ+ parented families in legislation, research, media, and society. A common thread within these publications included the positioning of LGBTQ+ parented families as 'not in the best interest of healthy child development' (Morgan, 2002) – echoed by and reflecting the tropes of recent media debates on LGBTQ+ parents discussed in the first chapter of this book. Arguments raised by these publications include the questioning of the ability of LGBTQ+ parents to offer family environments and contexts that contribute to well-adjusted child development, moralistic and religious arguments around the sanctity of dual-gendered parented families and highlighting of a range of potential 'risks' associated with children in the custody of LGBTQ+ parents (Cameron, 2006; Cameron & Cameron, 1996; Morgan, 2002; Schumm, 2010; van Gend, 2016).

Peer-reviewed articles such as Cameron (2006) and Schumm (2010) posited that LGBTQ+ parented families posed several risks factors for well-adjusted child development. These risks were supposed to have included a greater likelihood of children being victims of incest, sexual abuse, social/psychological maladjustment and 'sexual orientation transmission'. Following on from the research arguments made in the 1960s and 1970s papers, these authors commonly argued that LGBTQ+ parented families may not offer children 'appropriate' gender role models, could potentially cause gender or sexual orientation confusion in children and place children at risk of a range of developmental maladjustments. Commonly, these works were written in response to the growing body of empirical evidence highlighting a lack of difference between developmental outcomes of children parented by LGBTQ+ and heterosexual individuals (e.g. Patterson, 2006). This type of research drew on assumptions arising in the 1970s that homosexuality is an unnatural expression of sexual orientation and is a learned behaviour which involves the 'grooming' of children by predatory homosexual adults (Cameron & Cameron, 1996). These works are not commonly referred to in most peer-reviewed academic literature. They positioned LGBTQ+ identities as deficits to healthy child development, failed to include evidence drawn from LGBTQ+ participants, and included explicit bias in their homophobic and transphobic framings (Hicks, 2005; Stacey & Biblarz, 2001).

Grey literature similarly contains arguments against LGBTQ+ parented families and was written in response to increasingly progressive and equal treatment of LGBTQ+ parented families in policy, legislation, and social attitudes (e.g., Morgan, 2002; van Gend, 2016). Unlike peer-reviewed articles, these works included arguments against the 'far-left' LGBTQ+ social and political movements, that were largely portrayed as a potential threat to traditional patriarchal forms of the family (van Gend, 2016). Moralistic and religious sentiments in the literature, which are more difficult to critique, included the unnatural non-generative nature of LGBTQ+ parental units, the deprivation of children knowing their mothers and fathers, and the use of children as political pawns in a 'far-left' political agenda (Morgan, 2002; van Gend, 2016). This body of research tended to include misleading empirical research to justify its arguments against LGBTQ+ parented families. In common with peer-reviewed articles and anti-LGBTQ+ research in the 1950s and 1960s, these works typically failed to draw on empirical research exploring LGBTQ+ parented families *specifically*. For example, as part of her argument against LGBTQ+ parented families, Morgan (2002) drew on research exploring the health and wellbeing of LGBTQ+ youth and cited the alarming statistics related to suicidal behaviour, drug-use, and self-harm as evidence of the unsuitability of LGBTQ+ parents (not actually studied)... overlooking the contextual influences of structural and social homophobia and transphobia as factors in LGBTQ+ youth's poor outcomes (Hillier et al., 2010; Jones, 2015; Smith et al., 2014).

There have been several other limitations highlighted in this area of research. This research has commonly been authored by known affiliates to conservative Anti-LGBTQ+ religious institutions such as the Christian Concern, Australian Marriage Forum, Family Research Institute and Christian Institute (CCFON LTD, 2019; van Gend, 2019). As such, authors such as Hicks (2005) noted authors in these types of 'research papers' utilised anecdotal evidence supporting pre-existing anti-LGBTQ+ sentiments, heavily swayed by their admitted religious beliefs and so-called 'moral' rather than scientific ontologies. Limitations of this body of research include similar concerns to research in the 1960s–1970s in that little research explored LGBTQ+ parents specifically, and studies were critiqued for the misreporting and misrepresentation of results (Canadian Psychological Association (CPA) Board of Directors, 1996; Hicks, 2005). Additionally, we argue this anti-LGBTQ+ parent research appears to not only falsify or cherry-pick the negative findings it sets out to create; it can misrepresent the potential for psychological research to make a contribution *supportive* of LGBTQ+ parents or identities and turn some LGBTQ+ people off of seeking psychological and other potentially beneficial mental health supports included in school environments (Jones & Lasser, 2017). The papers' moralistic arguments that claim to draw on 'common sense' anecdotal evidence have also been noted to re-emerge in harmful ways for LGBTQ+ rights movements during debates around amendments to marriage equality laws (Knight et al., 2017), LGBTQ+ inclusive school curriculums (Ferfolja & Ullman, 2017), and religious views held by educators (Robinson, 2002).

2.3 LGBTQ+ parent and child development studies

LGBTQ+ parent and child development studies emerged in the 1970s–1980s+, exploring different aspects of psychological and social development of LGBTQ+ parented children. This body of literature commonly developed in response to assumptions in the 1960s and 1970s that LGBTQ+ identities were an illness, taboo, illegal and a potential threat to healthy child development. As a result of the predominant negative views of LGBTQ+ identities in medical, political and judicial environments, LGBTQ+ parents experienced unique challenges in being awarded custody of their children. Again, judicial systems largely viewed LGBTQ+ family and home contexts as 'not in the best interest of the child' (Beargie, 1988).

Researchers at the time noted judicial judgements included a range of justifications for not awarding custody to LGBTQ+ parents based on concerns around assumptions of parent lifestyle choices, promiscuity, social circles, and a-typical gender role behaviours (Bradley, 1987). Such family environments were often assumed to be related to adverse developmental outcomes in children. Associations were assumed with outcomes such as cognitive impairment, gender and sexual orientation confusion, social isolation and victimisation, and general maladjusted developmental trajectories (Beargie, 1988; Bradley, 1987; Kleber et al., 1986). In response to these adverse judicial decisions, a new body of evidence emerged, directly testing these assumptions through empirical evidence comparing the developmental outcomes and characteristics of children parented by heterosexual and LGBTQ+ adults (Anderssen et al., 2002; Golombok & Tasker, 1994; Lambert, 2005). Developmental outcomes assessed in these studies included gender role norms, gender identity, psychological adjustment, social functioning, sexual orientation and quality of parent-child relationships (Anderssen et al., 2002; Tasker, 2005; Tasker & Patterson, 2007).

Gender norms/roles are behaviours exhibited by individuals that are culturally accepted as masculine or feminine, while gender identity relates to the degree that a person identifies as male or female (Anderssen et al., 2002). Common methods employed in this gender norms research explored a child's preference in toys, play activities, clothes, career aspirations, television shows and contentment in 'born gender' (Bos & Sandfort, 2010; Goldberg & Garcia, 2016; Golombok et al., 1983; Gottman, 1990; Green, 1978; Green et al., 1986; Hoeffer, 1981). The consensus of this research was that the gender identity and gender norms of children of LGBTQ+ parents did not differ significantly when compared to heterosexual parented children (Bos & Sandfort, 2010; Goldberg & Garcia, 2016; Golombok et al., 1983; Gottman, 1990; Green, 1978; Green et al., 1986; Hoeffer, 1981). However, while not deleterious to children's adjustment, female children of lesbian parents were more likely than those of heterosexual parents to express interest in career aspirations (then) denoted as masculine including becoming astronauts, doctors and lawyers (Anderssen et al., 2002; Dempsey,

2013; Green et al., 1986). In more contemporary times, these career aspirations are no longer viewed as exclusively masculine career choices and highlight the highly temporal, cultural, and social bounds of 'typical' gender norms generally. These parent and child papers could in some ways be argued to have thus operated on cisnormative and sexist premises, seeing (or strategically speaking to, but therefore somewhat endorsing) beliefs in the inherent value in gender norms maintenance.

The psychological adjustment refers to a range of psychological development characteristics including an individuals' intelligence, behavioural problems, emotional functioning, school adjustment, self-concept, and moral judgements (Anderssen et al., 2002; Tasker & Patterson, 2007). As is the case with gender identity and gender role behaviours, studies of adjustment reported no statistical difference between heterosexual or LGBTQ+ parented children (Chan et al., 1998; Farr, 2017; Flaks et al., 1995; Golombok et al., 2013; Kirkpatrick, Smith & Roy, 1981; Vanfraussen et al., 2002; Wainwright, Russell & Patterson, 2004). Social functioning research relates to the quality of relationships and peer victimisation children experience in social contexts (Lambert, 2005). The studies of social functioning found no difference in ratings of popularity or peer group relationships between children of heterosexual or lesbian parented families (Freedman et al., 2002; Golombok & Tasker, 1994; MacCallum & Golombok, 2004; Vanfraussen et al., 2002). Research on bullying of LGBTQ+ parented children generally indicated that they were no more likely to be teased, harassed, or assaulted by peers when compared to heterosexual parented children (Freedman et al., 2002; Golombok & Tasker, 1994; Vanfraussen et al., 2002). However, children of LGBTQ+ parents were more likely to experience bullying related to the LGBTQ+ status of their parents and assumptions of themselves being LGBTQ+ (Ray & Gregory, 2001; Vanfraussen et al., 2002; Wyers, 1987). It may be problematic valuing social wellbeing and lack of bullying of children by other children as a 'measure of parenting', in that being bullied can be well beyond parental and individual control and not a reflection of inherent bad status but of social biases or lack of anti-bullying efforts for example.

Sexual orientation studies have explored whether children raised by LGBTQ+ parents were more likely to rate attraction to members of the same or opposite sex when compared to children reared by heterosexual parents (Anderssen et al., 2002; Golombok & Tasker, 1994; Gottman, 1990; Tasker, 2005). Contrary to anti-LGBTQ+ parent research anecdotes (e.g. Cameron, 2006), LGBTQ+ parents do not increase the likelihood of LGBTQ+ identifications in their children

(Allen & Burrell, 1997; Anderssen et al., 2002; Tasker, 2005). Rather, children of LGBTQ+ parents may be more open-minded about possibilities or 'trialling' same-sex relationships; rather than *identifying* as LGBTQ+ (Tasker & Patterson, 2007). More recent research on LG-BTQ+ parented families no longer explores this aspect of child development, arguing such enquiries are heterosexist: positioning sexual orientation and gender identity/expression diversity as a non-desirable developmental outcome (Short et al., 2007).

Parental-child relationship studies have compared heterosexual and LGBTQ+ parents' parent-child relationships to address assumptions that LGBTQ+ parents are 'unfit' parental figures for children (Tasker, 2005). Most of this research has identified that LGBTQ+ parents do not significantly differ from heterosexual parents in terms of parenting styles and quality of parent-child relationships (Golombok et al., 1983; Vanfraussen et al., 2002; Wainright et al., 2004). Indeed, LGBTQ+ parents may offer unique advantages in rearing children. For example, children of lesbian parents are more likely than children of heterosexual parents to rate greater levels of attachment with their parents, discuss emotional and sexual issues with their parents and perceive their parents as dependable (Golombok et al., 1997; MacCallum & Gollombok, 2004; Vanfraussen et al., 2002). Generally, these authors have concluded that family characteristics, processes and experiences shared by all types of parents and families, such as life stressors, were more predictive of the psychological adjustment of children rather than a parent's sexual orientation, gender identity or expression (Farr, 2017; Golombok et al., 2013; Wainwright et al., 2004).

These reoccurring findings of no statistical difference in empirical research comparing *negative* developmental outcomes and family relationships between LGBTQ+ and heterosexual parented children have been termed the 'no statistical difference consensus' (Stacey & Biblarz, 2001). This research is still contested by some researchers (e.g., Cameron, 1996; Marks, 2020; Schumm, 2010) for its small sample sizes; predominant representation of affluent, well-educated Caucasian lesbian parents; limited scope of developmental outcomes and little longitudinal data. Other critiques of this research include its positioning of heterosexual parents as the 'gold-star' for well-adjusted child development (Lambert, 2005), and the lack of recognition of environmental factors, such as stigmatising and discriminatory events, which may be more influential in healthy well-adjusted child development (Crouch et al., 2014; Knight et al., 2017). Rather, researchers have argued the need for studies to explore societal influences in parent and family wellbeing such as cultural and societal attitudes, legislative contexts, and the everyday experiences of LGBTQ+ parents navigating these environments (Lambert, 2005; Tasker, 2005). We have added our own points to this list of critique, our concern that some parenting measures used in some of these studies inherently valued cisnormative development, sexist conceptualisations of employment goals and spurious social ideals like a lack of one's child experiencing bullying by other children that forget contextual influences.

2.4 LGBTQ+ parented family diversity and family functioning studies

LGBTQ+ parented family diversity and family functioning studies emerged during the nineties, coinciding with societal, policy, legislative and medicalised framings that were more affirming of LGBTQ+ identities. In recognition of the relative lack of research exploring LGBTQ+ parents' every-day lives, this research set out to explore their home life characteristics and experiences in social contexts at times incorporating sociological lenses (Perlesz & McNair, 2004; Power et al., 2010). Researchers in this area aimed to gain descriptive statistics of family formations, identify LGBTQ+ parents' pathways to parenthood and explore their experiences in different contexts (e.g. school settings, health care providers, peer/family relationships) as a method to inform social organisations and professionals of the unique characteristics and needs of LGBTQ+ parents and their families (McNair et al., 2002; Rawsthorne, 2009; van Dam, 2004). Family functioning research has developed from the contribution of multiple disciplines and theoretical frameworks including critical psychological (Power et al., 2010) and queer and feminist lenses (Gabb, 2005) in qualitative (Rawsthorne, 2009) and quantitative (Power et al., 2010) research designs. This type of research is particularly privileged in developed countries such as Australia (Dempsey, 2013), U.S.A (Goldberg et al., 2014) and U.K. (Gabb, 2005). Commonly, the research indicates that LGBTQ+ parented families are unique in terms of demographic statistics (Australian Bureau of Statistics/ABS, 2016; Gates, 2013), methods of family formation (Power et al., 2010) and challenges experienced within social organisations and social networks (McNair et al., 2002; Rawsthorne, 2009).

Census data in Australia indicates LGBTQ+ parented families are a growing minority group (ABS, 2013, 2016). Current estimates indicate around 10,500 children are being raised by same-sex parents within Australia (ABS, 2017), compared to around seven million in the US (Gates, 2013). Although the actual number of LGBTQ+ parents are argued to be larger in countries such as Australia as national census surveys do not commonly include explicit measures of sexual orientation or gender diversity, and estimates are drawn from same-sex parents within current relationships that may overlook other parental characteristics such being single, divorced or co-parenting in separate households (ABS, 2013; Power et al., 2010). Aside from methodological concerns, LGBTQ+ parents may also be reticent to disclose information relating to their sexual orientation or gender identity in formal government surveys, as it has been noted parents may have apprehensions around drawing unwanted official attention or potential negative backlash to their family (ABS, 2016; Casper et al., 1992).

Generally, Australian data indicates that LGBTQ+ parents are more likely to earn higher incomes and attain higher levels of education compared to national samples (ABS, 2016; Power et al., 2010). Although some researchers contest whether this is a unique characteristic generalisable to the entire population of LGBTQ+ parented families or only representatives of those who participate in research (Perlesz et al., 2010). In contrast, demographic statistics in the US indicate same-sex parents earn lower incomes compared to national samples (Gates, 2013). Similar to heterosexual parented families, LGBTQ+ parent family research indicates the majority of families uphold traditional two-parent nuclear family formations or single parenting status (Power et al., 2010, 2012). However, studies exploring LGBTQ+ forms of family constellations have also noted more dynamic forms of family structures, including co-parenting/blended family formations between more than two actively engaged parents (Power et al., 2010). These family demographics can potentially include family formations involving parents who identify as lesbian female and gay male partnerships (and their same-sex partners) as well as family constellations that recognise known biological donors as adults responsible for the care of children (Dempsey, 2010; Power et al., 2010, 2012). Families that seek parenthood through the use of donor materials may acknowledge and include known donors as adults who are active within the lives of children as parental-like figures, or special friends of the family, or conversely may use anonymous donors that may not be included within the lives of the family (Dempsey, 2010, 2013). Common reasoning for maintaining relationships with donors include ensuring children's needs regarding questions about family and genetic history are met as a child develops, whilst anonymous donors were selected to overcome concerns of future personal and legal difficulties in terms of custody and access to children (Dempsey, 2010).

Unlike heterosexual parented families, LGBTQ+ parented families are commonly unable to experience unplanned pregnancies and may require the assistance of others in forming families (Mitchell &Green, 2008). Generally, research indicates a shift in methods of conception away from the historical assumptions of LGBTQ+ parents achieving parenthood through previous heterosexual relationships, to LGBTQ+ couples employing planned methods of parenthood via informal and formal sources of parenthood (Crouch et al., 2014; Power et al., 2010).

Identified methods of forming families include conception within previous heterosexual relationships, surrogacy agreements, Artificial Reproduction Technologies (ART) and fostering/adoption arrangements (Power et al., 2010; Short et al., 2007). Australian research indicates LGBTQ+ parents are more likely to prefer conceiving children where there is a biological relation between the child and parent (e.g., surrogacy, conception with donor assistance) over the adoption/foster care arrangements reported in the US (Crouch et al., 2014; Dempsey, 2013; Gates, 2013; Power et al., 2010).

Research exploring parents' intentions to seek parenthood has found that more affirmative changes to national and state laws (e.g. marriage equality and lifting of bans on adoption) may lead to adults having greater intentions of seeking parenthood (Goldberg et al., 2013). As reproductive technologies are becoming readily available at cheaper prices with recognition of LGBTQ+ parented families as applicable forms of family diversity in child placement and reproductive services, greater numbers of LGBTQ+ parented families may be expected within Australia (Hill et al., 2020). Although, intentions for parenthood may not lead to actual parent status. This also depends on state legislation granting access of LGBTQ+ adults to reproductive technologies and foster/adoption services (Dempsey, 2013), parent concerns around raising children in heterosexist contexts, costs of reproductive technologies and parent concerns of stigmatising experiences from reproductive technology services (Hill et al., 2020).

Family functioning research has also explored the challenging and supportive nature of LGBTQ+ parented families with informal (family of origin, peer networks) and formal (schools, health professionals) sources of support (Gabb, 2005; Mcnair et al., 2008; Mitchell &Green, 2008; Perlesz & McNair, 2004; Power et al., 2010; Rawsthorne, 2009). Generally, the research indicates the majority of LGBTQ+ parented families are privileged in the support of families of origin, which has been attributed to a greater likelihood of seeking parenthood and perceived support (Riggs et al., 2016). Common themes in the literature indicate parenthood may bond LGBTQ+ individuals with their families of origin, where their new predominant identity becomes that of a parent rather than an LGBTQ+ individual (McNair et al., 2002).

Although not all LGBTQ+ parents experience the support of their parents, with themes of lack of recognition of alternative pathways of seeking conception and illegitimacy of LGBTQ+ parents who may not be genetically related to their children (Rawsthorne, 2009; Power et al., 2012).

Research exploring the transition of LGBTQ+ adults to parents has found LGBTQ+ parented families experience similar levels of stress to heterosexual parented families upon becoming parents, with a noted shift of peer networks from predominantly LGBTQ+ social circles and community involvement to fellow parent social groups (McNair et al., 2002; Perlesz et al., 2006). In the case of weak informal sources of support or social networks such as the family of origin, or connections to LGBTQ+ communities, formal sources of support (such as schools) may be particularly important in providing protective strategies and connections to informal sources of support (Mcnair et al., 2008; Rawsthorne, 2009).

Studies on the experiences of LGBTQ+ parents interacting with potential sources of support such as education providers, childcare and professional health services indicate LGBTQ+ parented families experience unique challenges in interacting within contexts outside of the family (Rawsthorne, 2009; van Dam, 2004). Research of this type has identified common barriers in public service environments. These include: knowledge gaps in public service professionals relating to LGBTQ+ parented family formations (Eliason, 1996; Gahan, 2018), lack of policy and procedures inclusive of LGBTQ+ parented families (Eliason, 1996; Perlesz et al., 2006) and concerns of potential negative backlash from disclosing sexual orientation/ gender identity to public service personnel (Rawsthorne, 2009; van Dam, 2004). As family experiences of stigma and discrimination have been related to negative health and wellbeing (Crouch et al., 2014), common suggestions for service providers and researchers include developing policies and procedures that are inclusive of LGBTQ+ parented families (Power et al., 2010; Rawsthorne, 2009), and exploration of methods to protect LGBTQ+ parented families from stigmatising events within different contexts (Crouch et al., 2014). However, this research did not explore the school context in depth. This limited its ability to highlight LGBTQ+ parents' common experiences within school communities and the potential supportive role schools may play in LGBTQ+ parents' lives. The new study this book reports on in later chapters, addresses these gaps in research. It specifically explores LGBTQ+ parents' experiences within school communities and parents' views on a range of potential LGBTQ+ related school supports.

2.5 LGBTQ+ parents within schools studies

Studies explicitly focussing on LGBTQ+ parents within schools emerged in the 1990s due to rising recognition of the unique challenges that LGBTQ+ parented families faced in these environments. These challenges included the perpetuation of heterosexuality as 'normal' and the exclusion or 'othering' of LGBTQ+ identities (Casper et al., 1992; Gray et al., 2016). These studies have predominantly been based in the U.S.A. (Goldberg, Black, Manley, et al., 2017; Goldberg & Smith, 2014a, 2014b, 2017; Kosciw & Diaz, 2008; Leland, 2017), U.K. (McDonald & Morgan, 2019) and Australia (Cloughessy & Waniganayake, 2015; Cloughessy et al., 2018, 2019; Lindsay et al., 2006; Riggs & Willing, 2013). The theoretical lenses in these studies have been drawn from sociological and psychological disciplines including queer theory, post-modern theory, grounded theory, Foucaultian theory and psychological/ecological development frameworks utilising predominantly qualitative interview methodologies to explore experiences of LGBTQ+ parents in school environments (Cloughessy & Waniganayake, 2019; Cloughessy et al., 2018, 2019; Goldberg, Black, Sweeney, et al., 2017; Leland, 2017; Lindsay et al., 2006; Skattebol & Ferfolja, 2007).

To date, Abbie Goldberg from the U.S.A. (Goldberg, Black, Manley, et al., 2017; Goldberg & Smith, 2014a, 2014b, 2017) and Kathy Cloughessy from Australia (Cloughessy et al., 2018, 2019; Cloughessy & Waniganayake, 2015, 2019) have been the largest contributors to this body of research. Their work has focused on exploring various challenging and supportive factors LGBTQ+ parents experience in predominantly pre-school community contexts. From this research, various school characteristics have been associated with more positive and supportive school environments for LGBTQ+ parents. These factors have included location (Metropolitan vs. Remote areas; Lindsay et al., 2006), representation of diversity within school communities (Bower, 2008; Casper et al., 1992; Mcdonald & Morgan, 2019), local attitudes toward and representation of LGBTQ+ parented families (Casper et al., 1992; Goldberg, Black, Sweeney, et al., 2017; Goldberg & Smith, 2014a, 2014b; Lindsay et al., 2006), explicit inclusive school policy on family diversity (Kosciw & Diaz, 2008) and personal attitudes/ professional training of school personnel (Cloughessy et al., 2019; Goldberg, Black, Sweeney, et al., 2017).

Unlike other forms of diversity such as multiculturalism, some forms of special needs and some groups for whom English is a second language; sexual orientation and gender identity are unique forms of diversity in being largely invisible (Casper et al., 1992). This trait particularly requires either verbal disclosure, or secondary signaling such as the 'in-role' presence of significant others, for identification... which can nonetheless be misunderstood or unnoticed in ways occluding visibility. Commonly, schools are argued to reflect dominant family formations and social attitudes, which in the case of most developed countries denote traditional dual-gendered parented families (Casper et al., 1992; Kozik-Rosabal, 2000; Mercier & Harold, 2003). Schools endorse traditional forms of heterosexual families and suppress LGBTQ+ identities within their structures by explicitly not including LGBTQ+ parented families within school curriculum/ practices/pedagogical approaches and implicitly through the exclusive representation of heterosexual parented families (Casper et al., 1992; Fox, 2007; Ryan & Martin, 2000; UNESCO, 2016). Predominantly, previous research has explored LGBTQ+ parents' common experiences within school contexts including:

• how/why LGBTQ+ parents disclose their identity to school community members (Cloughessy et al., 2018; Goldberg, Black, Manley, et al., 2017; Lindsay et al., 2006);
• LGBTQ+ parent supportive and marginalising experiences within school environments (Bower, 2008; Casper et al., 1992; Cloughessy et al., 2019; Goldberg, 2014; Goldberg, Black, Manley et al., 2017; Goldberg & Smith, 2014b; Skattebol & Ferfolja, 2007);
• teacher/administrator perspectives on LGBTQ+ parented families (Cloughessy & Waniganayake, 2015; Ferfolja, 2007; Hegde et al., 2014; Robinson, 2002; Robinson & Ferfolja, 2001); and
• recommendations for best practice inclusive school support structures (Bower & Klecka, 2009; Fox, 2007; Goldberg, Black, Sweeney, et al., 2017; Mercier & Harold, 2003; Ryan & Martin, 2000).

The research shows not all LGBTQ+ parents disclose their sexual orientation and gender identity within schools (Casper et al., 1992; Jones et al., 2015). The decision to disclose family constellations varies depending on concerns of the individual and characteristics of the surrounding environment (Casper et al., 1992; Jones et al., 2015; Lindsay et al., 2006). LGBTQ+ parents that choose not to disclose their identity in schools generally relate to participants deeming family constellations and gender identities a private matter not relevant to schools, as protective measures against possible negative treatment toward children and parents from school community members (teachers, parents, administrators and other students) and concerns of family structures

becoming common knowledge within the local community or involvement of formal social services (Casper et al., 1992; Goldberg, 2014; Jones
et al., 2015; Lindsay et al., 2006).

Conversely, active disclosure of gender
identity and sexual orientation has been related to avoiding the burden
of identity management (McDonald & Morgan, 2019), ensuring school
staff are aware of the diversity within schools and meeting the needs of
students within classrooms (Casper et al., 1992; Cloughessy et al., 2018;
Riggs & Willing, 2013). There have also been aims to role-model pride
in family diversity to children (Cloughessy et al., 2018; Jones et al.,
2015; Lindsay et al., 2006), to create a response to marginalising school
practices that exclude LGBTQ+ forms of the family (Cloughessy et al.,
2018; Goldberg, Black, Manley, et al., 2017) and as a method of gaug-
ing school community stances on inclusivity when considering school
selection (Casper et al., 1992). A common finding in this research is all
LGBTQ+ parents ('out' or 'closeted') experience anxiety when considering disclosure (Casper et al., 1992; Cloughessy et al., 2018; Mercier &
Harold, 2003; Riggs & Willing, 2013). However, prospective parents are
more likely to perceive greater challenges within school systems, than
are actually experienced by LGBTQ+ parents in school communities
(Ray & Gregory, 2001).

Common methods of disclosure include altering school forms to
include diverse family constellations, verbal disclosure to teachers
and administrators, or more naturalistic methods including the active
involvement and visibility of various parents within their children's
schools (Casper et al., 1992; Cloughessy et al., 2018). Earlier research
indicated LGBTQ+ parents were more likely to adopt 'closeted' disclosure positions in schools (Casper et al., 1992; Lindsay et al., 2006;
McNair & Perlesz, 2004) compared to more recent research in the
last few years highlighting LGBTQ+ parents as mostly 'out' within
school contexts (Cloughessy et al., 2019; Goldberg, Black, Sweeney,
et al., 2017; Leland, 2017; Mcdonald & Morgan, 2019). This potentially
reflects changing social attitudes and legal rights acknowledging and
accepting of LGBTQ+ identities. However, this research is typically
privileged in countries that may have more affirming views of LG-
BTQ+ identities in recent laws, social attitudes and policies potentially
limiting the generalisability of findings and themes to more hostile, or
less privileged national/regional contexts.

Identified challenges in schools include:

• lack of recognition of LGBTQ+ parented families as valid forms
  of family from school community members (teachers, school staff,
  other parents and students; (Cloughessy et al., 2019; Lindsay et al.,
  2006; Riggs & Willing, 2013),

- lack of inclusive language within school classrooms and school forms that may exclude children with families not consisting of dual-gendered parents (Cloughessy et al., 2019; Goldberg, 2014),
- experiences of homophobia and transphobia by school community members (Kosciw & Diaz, 2008; Lindsay et al., 2006; Ray & Gregory, 2001),
- lack of representation of LGBTQ+ families or individuals within school environments (Casper et al., 1992; Ryan & Martin, 2000),
- assumptions of teachers that students of LGBTQ+ parents may be LGBTQ+ or experience behavioural difficulties (similar to assumptions made in anti-LGBTQ+ studies; Casper et al., 1992; Cloughessy et al., 2019), and
- general 'clumsiness' in school personnel around addressing LGBTQ+ parent family structures inclusively (Cloughessy et al., 2018; Goldberg et al., 2017).

Whilst research is limited on the experiences of LGBTQ+ parents in schools, more recent research tends to indicate a minority of participants experienced negative or discriminatory events (Cloughessy et al., 2019; Farr et al., 2016). However, there are noted concerns around the representativeness of these findings to the LGBTQ+ population with most research being drawn from lesbian Caucasian mothers in small samples of convenience. This is a limitation that generally applies to all LGBTQ+ parent research, in some ways reflecting the greater access lesbians have to fertility treatments and arrangements as women.

Positive experiences in education generally include proactive or reactive measures taken by schools to accommodate LGBTQ+ parented families (Cloughessy et al., 2019a; Leland, 2017). These supportive strategies include:

- inclusive language and differentiated classroom activities for students of LGBTQ+ parents particularly during traditional family celebration days (e.g. Mother's Day and Father's Day; Cloughessy et al., 2019a; Goldberg, Black, Sweeney, et al., 2017),
- discussions between parent/s and schools on how to approach/ accommodate diverse family structures in classroom activities (Bower, 2008; Cloughessy et al., 2019),
- inclusive language and classroom activities that include LGBTQ+ topics/issues alongside other forms of family diversity as part of the curriculum (Bower, 2008; Goldberg et al., 2017),
- schools that value diversity represented within the school community and school-related committees (Goldberg & Smith, 2014; Leland, 2017), and

• representation of other LGBTQ+ parented families and staff within school communities (Farr et al., 2016; McDonald & Morgan, 2019).

Researchers also note that parents are not passive in their child(ren)'s educational environments and attempt to actively engage with schools to address the potential exclusion or lack of representation of family constellations such as their own (Riggs & Willing, 2013; Skattebol & Ferfolja, 2007). Identified strategies adopted by LGBTQ+ parents include participation in policy development, school committees, selection of schools that value diversity, and the donation of age-appropriate learning materials (such as books and other objects) in an effort to 'normalise' LGBTQ+ parented families amongst other forms of diversity (Goldberg & Smith, 2014b; Leland, 2017; Skattebol & Ferfolja, 2007). The active efforts of parents to create change within their child(ren)'s schools have largely been employed to overcome the lack of appropriate inclusive practices, and evident knowledge gaps in educational professionals – a phenomenon termed 'educating the educator' (Riggs & Willing, 2012). In recognition of the predominant reactive strategies in schools, where school practices and procedures have been noted to be adapted after the identification and presence of LGBTQ+ parents in school systems (Cloughessy & Waniganayake, 2015), some researchers have suggested parents disclose their sexual orientations or gender identities as a method to create change in their child(ren)'s schools (Casper et al., 1992). Other researchers have noted that such parent attempts at creating change through advocacy of their families have been met with various levels of marginalisation or denial depending on the stand of the school, school staff and local community (Riggs & Willing, 2013). Arguments for parent-advocacy and parent-led activities for change in schools may be a particularly relevant strategy to adopt in national contexts which privilege greater recognition, acknowledgement, and legislative protections for LG-BTQ+ identities generally. However, we note an issue with this body of research is that sometimes the complexities of international trans-ferability of data are not considered. Activist actions may prove more difficult for parents located in less affirming environments and con-texts, with the potential for backlash, ostracisation, the involvement of family or social services, and exclusion from educational systems (Casper et al., 1992; UNESCO, 2016).

Research on LGBTQ+ parents in school contexts has highlighted a wealth of information concerning the challenges and inclusive experiences parents derive from educational environments. Yet, little research has explored LGBTQ+ parents' views on how they would like to be systematically included or represented within school contexts. Recent researchers have argued that the growing number of countries legalising same-sex marriage and marriage equality highlights the need for the development of LGBTQ+ inclusive educational policies, and empirical research to inform the development of such policies (Liang & Cohrssen, 2020). We would say this gap in the literature is further justified by the trend towards outness in educational environments for LGBTQ+ parents; which makes it likely older strategies of serving their needs foregrounding institutional silence (don't ask, don't tell) may no longer so consistently apply. To meet this gap in literature, this study presents LGBTQ+ parents' views and perspectives on common inclusive school strategies endorsed by literature (e.g., LGBTQ+ inclusive curriculums and teacher training in LGBTQ+ topics).

2.6 Summary of key points

The key points that can be summarised for this chapter include:

- Anti-LGBTQ+ family studies in the 1960s, 1970s and 1990s were heavily influenced by cultural/religious beliefs and medicalised lenses casting LGBTQ+ identities as illegal, taboo and disordered. Common arguments derived from questionable data, or *mere opinion*, that family structures excluding gendered role-models created children's mental disorders, homosexuality, and gender confusion.
- Child development studies in the 1980s+ commonly affirmed LGBTQ+ parents as making 'no statistical difference' to children's development, however they often inherently valued cisnormative, heteronormative, sexist or otherwise problematic measures and overlooked contextual factors.
- Family functioning research in the 1990s+ found LGBTQ+ families included various adults gaining parenthood status via a variety of ways.
- School context studies showed LGBTQ+ parents can find schools challenging environments, and had more positive experiences where:
  - staff are trained in LGBTQ+ topics, issues or families,
  - procedures/communications don't stress gendered wording,
  - teaching practices and resources are inclusive of LGBTQ+ families, and
  - diversity is broadly conceived.

2.7 Conclusion & next chapters

This chapter explored anti-LGBTQ+ research (and their critiques), research exploring the developmental outcomes of children parented by LGBTQ+ parents (and their challenges), and family functioning and education context studies (and their gaps). The review identified strengths and challenges schools can pose in the lives of LGBTQ+ parented families and the need for the new LGBTQ+ parent study at the core of this book. The next chapter discusses the theoretical lenses, research questions and methodology applied within this study.

References

ABS. (2013). *410.2.0 Australian Social Trends, July 2013.* Retrieved from: www.abs.gov.au

ABS. (2016). *6224.055 Labour force, Australia: Labour Force Status and Other Characteristics of Families.* Retrieved from: www.abs.gov.au

ABS. (2017). *2071.0- Census of Population and Housing: Reflecting Australia - Stories from the Census, 2016.* Retrieved from: www.abs.gov.au

Allen, M., & Burrell, N. (1997). Comparing the impact of homosexual and heterosexual parents on children. *Journal of Homosexuality, 32*(2), 19–35.

Anderssen, N., Amlie, C., & Ytterøy, E. A. (2002). Outcomes for children with lesbian or gay parents. *Scandinavian Journal of Psychology, 43*(4), 335–351.

APA. (1952). *Diagnostic and Statistical Manual of Mental Disorders.* Washington: APA.

APA. (1968). *Diagnostic and Statistical Manual of Mental Health Disorders* (2nd ed., text rev.). Washington: APA.

Beargie, R. (1988). Custody determinations involving the homosexual parent. *Family Law Quarterly, 22*(1), 71–86.

Bene, E. (1965). On the genesis of male homosexuality. *The British Journal of Psychiatry, 111*(478), 803–813.

Bieber, I. (1962). *Homosexuality.* London: Basic Books.

Bos, H., & Sandfort, T. (2010). Children's gender identity in lesbian and heterosexual two-parent families. *Sex Roles, 62*(2), 114–126.

Bower, L. (2008). Standing up for diversity. *Kappa Delta Pi Record, 44*(4), 181–183.

Bower, L., & Klecka, C. (2009). (Re)considering normal. *Teaching Education, 20*(4), 357–373.

Bradley, D. (1987). Homosexuality and child custody in English Law. *International Journal of Law and the Family, 1*(2), 155.

Cameron, P. (2006). Children of homosexuals and transsexuals more apt to be homosexual. *Journal of Biosocial Science, 38*(3), 413–418.

Cameron, P., & Cameron, K. (1996). Homosexual parents. *Adolescence, 31*(124), 757–776.

Casper, V., Schultz, S., & Wickens, E. (1992). Breaking the silences. *Teachers College Record, 94*(1), 109–137.

CCFON LTD. (2019). *Christian Concern*. Retrieved from https://www.christianconcern.com/

Chan, R., Brooks, R., Raboy, B., & Patterson, C. (1998). Division of labor among lesbian and heterosexual parents. *Journal of Family Psychology, 12*(2), 443–457.

Cloughessy, K., & Waniganayake, M. (2015). "Raised eyebrows". *Children & Society, 29*(5), 377–387.

Cloughessy, K., & Waniganayake, M. (2019). Lesbian parents' perceptions of children's picture books featuring same-sex parented families. *Early Years, 39*(2), 118–131.

Cloughessy, K., Waniganayake, M., & Blatterer, H. (2018). "This is our family. We do not hide who we are". *Journal of GLBT Family Studies, 14*(4), 381–399.

Cloughessy, K., Waniganayake, M., & Blatterer, H. (2019). The good and the bad. *Journal of Research in Childhood Education, 33*(3), 446–458.

CPA Board of Directors. (1996, August 01). *Policy Statement*. Retrieved from: https://cpa.ca/aboutcpa/policystatements/#cameron

Crouch, S. R., Waters, E., McNair, R., Power, J., & Davis, E. (2014). Parent-reported measures of child health and wellbeing in same-sex parent families. *BMC Public Health, 14*(1), 635–635.

Dempsey, D. (2010). Conceiving and negotiating reproductive relationships. *Sociology, 44*(6), 1145–1162.

Dempsey, D. (2013). Same-sex parented families in Australia. *Australian Institute of Family Studies (18)*, 1–26. Retrieved from: https://aifs.gov.au/cfca/publications/same-sex-parented-families-australia

Drescher, J. (2015). Out of DSM. *Behavioral Sciences, 5*(4), 565–575.

Drescher, J., & Byne, W. (2012). Gender dysphoric/gender variant (GD/GV) children and adolescents. *Journal of Homosexuality, 59*(3), 501–510.

Eliason, M. J. (1996). Lesbian and gay family issues. *Journal of Family Nursing, 2*(1), 10–29.

Evans, R. B. (1969). Childhood parental relationships of homosexual men. *Journal of Consulting and Clinical Psychology, 33*(2), 129–135.

Farr, R. (2017). Does parental sexual orientation matter? *Developmental Psychology, 53*(2), 252–264.

Farr, R. H., Oakley, M. K., & Ollen, E. W. (2016). School experiences of young children and their lesbian and gay adoptive parents. *Psychology of Sexual Orientation and Gender Diversity, 3*(4), 442–447.

Ferfolja, T. (2007). Schooling cultures. *International Journal of Inclusive Education, 11*(2), 147–162.

Ferfolja, T., & Ullman, J. (2017). Gender and sexuality in education and health. *Sex Education* 17(3), 235–241.

Flaks, D., Ficher, I., Masterpasqua, F., & Joseph, G. (1995). Lesbians choosing motherhood. *Developmental Psychology, 31*(6), 105–114.

Fox, R. K. (2007). One of the hidden diversities in schools. *Childhood Education, 83*(5), 277–281.

Gabb, J. (2005). Locating lesbian parent families. *Gender, Place and Culture, 12*(4), 419–432.

Gahan, L. (2018). Separated same-sex parents. *Sociological Research Online*, 23(1), 245–261.

Gates, G. J. (2013). *LGBT Parenting in the United States*. Los Angeles: Williams Institute.

Goldberg, A. E. (2014). Lesbian, gay, and heterosexual adoptive parents' experiences in preschool environments. *Early Childhood Research Quarterly*, 29(4), 669–681.

Goldberg, A. E., Black, K., Sweeney, K., & Moyer, A. (2017). Lesbian, gay, and heterosexual adoptive parents' perceptions of inclusivity and receptiveness in early childhood education settings. *Journal of Research in Childhood Education*, 31(1), 141–159.

Goldberg, A. E., Black, K. A., Manley, M. H., & Frost, R. (2017). "We told them that we are both really involved parents". *Gender and Education*, 29(5), 614–631.

Goldberg, A. E., Gartrell, N., & Gates, G. J. (2014). *Research Report on LGBT-Parented Families*. Los Angeles: Williams Institute.

Goldberg, A. E., & Garcia, R. L. (2016). Gender-Typed behaviour over time in children with lesbian, gay, and heterosexual parents. *Journal of Family Psychology*, 30(7), 854–865.

Goldberg, A. E., Moyer, A. M., Weber, E. R., & Shapiro, J. (2013). What changed when the gay adoption ban was lifted? *Sexuality Research & Social Policy*, 10(2), 110–124.

Goldberg, A. E., & Smith, J. Z. (2014a). Perceptions of stigma and self-reported school engagement in same-sex couples with young children. *Psychology of Sexual Orientation and Gender Diversity*, 1(3), 202–212.

Goldberg, A. E., & Smith, J. Z. (2014b). Preschool selection considerations and experiences of school mistreatment among lesbian, gay, and heterosexual adoptive parents. *Early Childhood Research Quarterly*, 29(1), 64–75.

Goldberg, A. E., & Smith, J. Z. (2017). Parent-school relationships and young adopted children's psychological adjustment in lesbian, gay, and heterosexual-parent families. *Early Childhood Research Quarterly*, 40, 174–187.

Golombok, S., Mellish, L., Jennings, S., Casey, P., Tasker, F., & Lamb, M. (2013). Adoptive gay father families. *Child Development*, 456–468.

Golombok, S., Spencer, A., & Rutter, M. (1983). Children in Lesbian and single-parent households. *Journal of Child Psychology and Psychiatry*, 24(4), 551–572.

Golombok, S., & Tasker, F. (1994). Children in lesbian and gay families. *Annual Review of Sex Research*, 5(1), 73–100.

Golombok, S., Tasker, F., & Murray, C. (1997). Children raised in fatherless families from infancy. *Journal of Child Psychiatry and Applied Disciplines*, 38, 783–791.

Gonsiorek, J. (1982a). An Introduction to mental health issues and homosexuality. *The American Behavioral Scientist*, 25(4), 367–384.

Gonsiorek, J. (1982b). Results of psychological testing on homosexual populations. *The American Behavioral Scientist*, 25(4), 385–396.

Gottman, J. (1990). Children of gay and lesbian parents. In F. Bozzett, & M. Sussman (Eds.), *Homosexuality and family relations* (pp. 177–196). New York: Harrington Press.

Gray, E., Harris, A., & Jones, T. (2016). Australian LGBTQ teachers, exclusionary spaces and points of interruption. *Sexualities, 19*(3), 286–303.

Green, R. (1978). Sexual identity of 37 children raised by homosexual or transsexual parents. *American Journal of Psychiatry, 135*(2), 692–697.

Green, R., Mandel, J., Hotvedt, M., Gray, J., & Smith, L. (1986). Lesbian mothers and their children. *Archives of Sexual Behaviour, 15*(3), 167–184.

Hegde, A. V, Averett, P., Parker White, C., & Deese, S. (2014). Examining preschool teachers' attitudes, comfort, action orientation and preparation to work with children reared by gay and lesbian parents. *Early Child Development and Care, 184*(7), 963–976.

Herbstrith, J. C., Tobin, R. M., Hesson-McInnis, M. S., & Joel Schneider, W. (2013). Preservice teacher attitudes toward gay and lesbian parents. *School Psychology Quarterly, 28*(3), 183–194.

Hicks, S. (2005). Is gay parenting bad for kids? *Sexualities, 8*(2), 153–168.

Hill, A. O., Bourne, A., McNair, R., Carman, M., & Lyons, A. (2020). *Private Lives 3*. Melbourne: ARCSHS.

Hillier, L., Jones, T., Monagle, M., Overton, N., Gahan, L., Blackman, J., & Mitchell, A. (2010). *Writing Themselves In 3*. Melbourne: ARCSHS.

Hoeffer, B. (1981). Children's acquisitions of sex-role behaviour in lesbian-mother families. *American Journal of Orthopsychiatry, 22*(1), 536–544.

Jones, T. (2015). *Policy and Gay, Lesbian, Bisexual, Transgender and Intersex Students*. New York: Springer.

Jones, T., del Pozo de Bolger, A., Dunne, T., Lykins, A., & Hawkes, G. (2015). *Female-to-Male (FtM) Transgender People's Experiences in Australia*. London: Springer.

Jones, T., & Lasser, J. (2017). *School Psychology with Gay, Lesbian, Bisexual, Transgender, Intersex, and Questioning (GLBTIQ) Youth*. In M. Thielking & M. Terjesen (Eds.), Handbook On Australian School Psychology (pp. 595–612). Dordrecht: Springer.

Kirkpatrick, M., Smith, C., & Roy, R. (1981). Lesbian mothers and their children: A comparative survey. *American Journal of Orthopsychiatry, 51*(5), 3–11.

Kleber, D., Howell, R., & Tibbits-Kleber, A. (1986). The impact of parental homosexuality in child custody cases. *The Journal of the American Academy of Psychiatry and the Law, 14*(1), 81–101.

Knight, K. W., Stephenson, S. E., West, S., Delatycki, M. B., Jones, C. A., Little, M. H., Patton, G. C., Sawyer, S. M., Skinner, S. R., Telfer, M. M., Wake, M., North, K. N., & Oberklaid, F. (2017). The kids are OK. *Medical Journal of Australia, 207*(9), 374–375.

Kosciw, J. G., & Diaz, E. M. (2008). *Involved, Invisible, Ignored*. New York: GLSEN.

Kozik-Rosabal, G. (2000). "Well, we haven'tnoticed anything bad going on," said the principal. *Education and Urban Society, 32*(3), 368–389.

Lambert, S. (2005). Gay and lesbian families. *The Family Journal, 13*(1), 43–51.

Leland, A. (2017). Navigating gay fatherhood. *Gender and Education, 29*(5), 632–647.

Liang, X., & Cohrssen, C. (2020). Towards creating inclusive environments for LGBTIQparented families in early childhood education and care settings. *Australasian Journal of Early Childhood, 45*(1), 43–55.

Lindsay, J., Perlesz, A., Brown, R., McNair, R., De Vaus, D., & Pitts, M. (2006). Stigma or respect. *Sociology, 40*(6), 1059–1077.

MacCallum, F., & Golombok, S. (2004). Children raised in fatherless families. *Journal of Child Psychology and Psychiatry, 45*, 1407–1419.

Mcdonald, I., & Morgan, G. (2019). Same-sex parents' experiences of schools in England. *Journal of GLBT Family Studies, 15*(5), 486–500.

McNair, R., Brown, R., Perlesz, A., Lindsay, J., De Vaus, D., & Pitts, M. (2008). Lesbian parents negotiating the health care system in Australia. *Health Care for Women International, 29*(2), 91–114.

McNair, R., Dempsey, D., Wise, S., & Perlesz, A. (2002). Lesbian parenting. *Family Matters, 63*, 40–49.

McNair, R., & Perlesz, A. (2004). Lesbian parenting: insiders' voices. *Australian and New Zealand Journal of Family Therapy, 25*(3), 129–140.

Mercier, L. R., & Harold, R. D. (2003). At the interface. *Children & Schools, 25*(1), 35–47.

Mitchell, V., &Green, R. J. (2008). Different storks for different folks. *Journal of GLBT Family Studies, 3*(2–3), 81–104.

Morgan, P. (2002). *Children as Trophies?* New Castle upon Tyne: Christian Insititute.

Patterson, C. (2006). Children of lesbian and gay parents. *Current Directions in Psychological Science, 15*(5), 241–244.

Perlesz, A., Brown, R., Lindsay, J., McNair, R., De Vaus, D., & Pitts, M. (2006). Family in transition. *Journal of Family Therapy, 28*(2), 175–199.

Perlesz, A., & McNair, R. (2004). Lesbian parenting. *Australian and New Zealand Journal of Family Therapy, 25*(3), 129–140.

Perlesz, A., Power, J. B., McNair, R., Schofield, M., Pitts, M., Barrett, A., & Bickerdlike, A. (2010). Organising work and home in same-sex parented families: Findings from the work love play study. *The Australian and New Zealand Journal of Family Therapy*, 374–391.

Power, J., Perlesz, A., Brown, R., Schofield, M., Pitts, M., McNair, R., & Bickerdike, A. (2010). Diversity, tradition and family: Australian same-sex attracted parents and their families. *Gay and Lesbian Issues and Psychology Review, 6*(2), 66.

Power, J., Perlesz, A., Mcnair, R., Schofield, M., Pitts, M., Brown, R., & Bickerdike, A. (2012). Gay and bisexual dads and diversity. *Journal of Family Studies, 18*(2–3), 143–154.

Rawsthorne, M. L. (2009). Just like other families? *Australian Social Work, 62*(1), 45–60.

Ray, V., & Gregory, R. (2001). School experiences of the lesbian and gay. *Family Matters, 59*, 28–34.

Riggs, D. W., Power, J., & von Doussa, H. (2016). Parenting and Australian trans and gender diverse people. *The International Journal of Transgenderism, 17*(2), 59–65.

Riggs, D. W., & Willing, I. (2013). "They're all just little bits, aren't they". *Journal of Australian Studies, 37*(3), 364–377.

Robinson, K. (2002). Making the invisible visible. *Contemporary Issues in Early Childhood, 3*(3), 415–434.

Robinson, K., & Ferfolja, T. (2001). "What are we doing this for?". *British Journal of Sociology of Education, 22*(1), 121–133.

Ryan, D., & Martin, A. (2000). Lesbian, gay, bisexual, and transgender parents in the school systems. *School Psychology Review, 29*(2), 207–216.

Schumm, W. R. (2010). Children of homosexuals more apt to be homosexuals? *Journal of Biosocial Science, 42*(6), 721–742.

Short, E., Riggs, D., Perlesz, A., Brown, R., & Kane, G. (2007). *Lesbian, Gay, Bisexual, and Transgender Parented Families.* Melbourne: APS.

Smith, E., Jones, T., Ward, R., Dixon, J., Mitchell, A., & Hillier, L. (2014). *From Blues to Rainbows.* Melbourne: ARCSHS.

Skattebol, J., & Ferfolja, T. (2007). Voices from an enclave. *Australasian Journal of Early Childhood, 32*(1), 10–18.

Snortum, J. R., Mosberg, L., Marshall, J. E., Gillespie, J. F., & McLaughlin, J. P. (1969). Family dynamics and homosexuality. *Psychological Reports, 24*(3), 763–770.

Stacey, J., & Biblarz, T. (2001). (How) does the sexual orientation of parents matter? *American Sociological Review, 66*(2), 159–183.

Tasker, F. (2005). Lesbian mothers, gay fathers, and their children. *Journal of Developmental and Behavioral Pediatrics, 26*(3), 224–240.

Tasker, F., & Patterson, C. J. (2007). Research on Gay and Lesbian Parenting. *Journal of GLBT Family Studies, 3*(2–3), 9–34.

UNESCO. (2016). *Out In The Open.* Paris: UNESCO.

van Dam, M. A. A. (2004). Mothers in two types of lesbian families. *Journal of Family Nursing, 10*(4), 450–484.

van Gend, D. (2016). *Stealing From a Child.* Brisbane: Connor Court.

van Gend, D. (2019). Australian Marriage Forum. Brisbane: Australian Marriage Forum.

Vanfraussen, K., Ponjaert-Kristoffersen, I., & Brewaeys, A. (2002). What does it mean for youngsters to grow up in a lesbian family created by means of donor insemination?. *Journal of Reproductive and Infant Psychology, 20*(4), 237–252.

Wainright, J., Russell, S., & Patterson, C. (2004). Psychosocial adjustment, school outcomes, and romantic relationships of adolescents with same-sex parents. *Child Development, 75*(6), 1886–1898.

Wyers, N. (1987). Homosexuality in the family. *Social Work, 32*, 143–148.

3 Framing LGBTQ+ parents in theory, research & practice

LGBTQ+ parents reflect on: family structures vs. school structures
I don't have a lot of interaction with the school (...) it would be nice if they understood our family structure.

(Olivia, 30 yrs, New South Wales)

It is incredibly offensive to assume each family is made up of a mum and dad. We intentionally rewrite forms at our child's school.

(Ivy, 39 yrs, Vic)

We're basically talking about cultural safety here. I transitioned while my 2 youngest were in primary school. There was, to my knowledge, no education of or references to transgender (or same sex attracted) people. Consequently my kids were terrified of how their teachers and classmates would treat them. This is something that could have been avoided if these issues were openly discussed and my children were aware that ALL family structures are valued and accepted!

(Austin, 53 yrs, QLD)

I think we have educated our children's teachers, year by year, simply by our doggedly unsensational presence. Our school is not threatened by us, as we are one family structure of many. However, I am unsure whether all the school staff are as comfortable with us as I hope. Education would expose the cracks.

(Fran, 48 yrs, South Australia)

3.1 Introduction: lenses for viewing LGBTQ+ parents

Education structures in and beyond schools can struggle to accommodate LGBTQ+ family structures, because they are not based on thinking which theorises family in ways that go beyond heteronormative and cis-normative models. Similarly, the previous chapter argued

DOI: 10.4324/9781003167471-3

that some theoretical frames used for research on LGBTQ+ parents at their core do not imagine or affirm the possibility of framing anyone beyond cisgender and heterosexual individuals as inherently healthy, creating 'research' not even requiring direct engagement with LG-BTQ+ parents themselves in order to dismiss their value. The purpose of the first section of this third chapter is to discuss the inappropriateness of traditional and liberal psychological lenses to LGBTQ+ parent research. It then discusses some of the challenges posed by the interdisciplinary nature of LGBTQ+ parent research and the usefulness of critical social psychology lenses to consolidate and build upon the more valuable aspects of separate bodies of previous research. The chapter continues highlighting the potential for strength-based psychology in recognition of the predominant deficit model in this field of research. This chapter then discusses the potential for the Theory of Ecological Development (Bronfenbrenner, 1974; Bronfenbrenner & Crouter, 1983) as a potential framework applicable to LGBTQ+ parent research; as a means to fuse the more useful aspects of diverse interdisciplinary approaches that have explored various LGBTQ+ parent and family life in the literature – using Australian research as an exemplary case study. The chapter concludes by highlighting key points of the framework, and ends with reflections towards the next chapter.

3.2 Psychology's conceptualisations of LGBTQ+ parents

Chapter 2 highlighted previous examples of studies utilising traditional and liberal psychological lenses to LGBTQ+ samples. Moreover, it detailed some of their distinct limitations. Anti-LGBTQ+ Studies' in the 1960s+ utilised traditional psychological, psychoanalytic and aetiological lenses to explore family characteristics related to the development of homosexuality or gender identity disorders reflecting the classification of LGBTQ+ as symptomology of various mental health disorders (DSM-I; APA, 1952). This research highlighted several limitations and challenges in adopting medicalised or traditional methodologies to LGBTQ+ identities and samples, including potential pre-positioning of LGBTQ+ identities as a mental disorder, illness or disease and the potential for cultural and researcher-led bias (Drescher, 2015; Gonsiorek, 1982).

In the 1970s research saw increasing use of liberal psychological frameworks in Parent and Child Development Studies in recognition of the lack of research to resist assumptions that parent or adult role modelling of sexual orientations and gender identities led to maladaptive child development (Lambert, 2005). This research typically used some reliable and robust scientific measures of child development in studies comparing the developmental characteristics of cis-gendered heterosexual parented children to LGBTQ+ parented children (Anderssen et al., 2002). This comprehensive body of evidence has contributed to a range of beneficial outcomes for LGBTQ+ parents informing progressive legislative and policy changes recognising the rights of parents. However, we have noted distinct challenges to liberal psychological approaches in LGBTQ+ parent research including its implicit bias in positioning heterosexual parents as 'the gold star' for adaptive child development by privileging some cisnormative and heteronormative measures of 'good parenting outcomes'. Also, there have been critiques of its inability to account for experiences within larger social contexts which are argued to be more influential in family health and well-being (Knight et al., 2017; Lambert, 2005), and we noted that social contexts may directly affect other measures applied in the research like whether or not LGBTQ+ parents' children were bullied.

In recognition of the pathologising views of conservative psychological research in the 1960s and 1970s, LGBTQ+ parent literature saw an emerging shift in the 1990s to qualitative and mixed-methodological approaches in disciplines other than psychology (Bliss & Harris, 1998; Casper et al., 1992). Typically, this research utilised sociological theories of minority groups, sexuality and gender including Butler, queer theory, Foucault, feminist theory and post-modern theory to explore the everyday experiences of LGBTQ+ parents and their families (e.g. Cloughessy & Waniganayake, 2015; Gabb, 2005; McNair et al., 2002; Rawsthorne, 2009). This type of research has emerged as a prominent disciplinary approach in LGBTQ+ parent research. It may be a particularly culturally sensitive method of exploring the experiences of parents. Particularly, as researchers have noted, this sensitivity is important as parents may be reticent to disclose their identification as LGBTQ+ for fear of discrimination to themselves and their families (Casper et al., 1992), may have concerns around research findings and depictions of LGBTQ+ parents in media and research (Gahan, 2018), and further may reject the historical placement of LGBTQ+ identities in deficit theoretical models (e.g. anti-LGBTQ+ studies in the 1960s and 1970s).

Additionally, previous LGBTQ+ parent sociological research had identified several practical challenges and protective factors experienced by LGBTQ+ parents and families in school contexts. LGBTQ+ Parented Family Diversity and Family Functioning Studies, and LGBTQ+ Parents within Schools Studies have commonly aimed to generate empirical evidence drawn from LGBTQ+ minority groups to inform the development of LGBTQ+ inclusive professional practices, procedures and policies (e.g. Lindsay et al., 2006; Perlesz et al., 2010). Commonly, these studies utilised more affirming broad theorisation of LGBTQ+ parents through critical psychological lenses using post-modern, queer and feminist concepts of gender and sexuality as socially or discursively constructed (including in Gabb, 2005; Gray et al., 2016; Rawsthorne, 2009 and others). These studies have explored multiple facets of LGBTQ+ parents and their families including their interactions with social organisations (e.g. schools and medical health organisations) and informal social supports (e.g. relationships with the family of origin and memberships in the LGBTQ+ community) in recognition of their potential influence on LGBTQ+ parented families general health and well-being (McNair et al., 2002; Rawsthorne, 2009). Therefore, a critical social psychology framework may offer a more appropriate psychological lens combining elements of these studies' most useful contributions to the development of research exploring LGBTQ+ parents in school contexts.

3.3 Critical social psychology

Social psychology explores the influence of social contexts on an individual's development including factors such as mass media, family relationships and social organisations (i.e. schools); blending scientific methods with sociological lenses (DeLamatar et al., 2015). Critical social psychology developed from feminist and constructivist roots alongside social movements based on equality between classes, genders and races. It drew on how these sources recognised the lack of representation of minority groups in traditional psychological approaches (Gundlach, 2015; Worst & Smith, 2017). Critical social psychology commonly rejects traditional or conservative approaches to psychology; framing these approaches as potentially excluding the perspectives of underrepresented minority groups, perpetuating deficit (or problematic) framings of minority groups, and positioning minority groups (such as LGBTQ+ identities, as shown in the previous chapter) as 'abnormal' (Gundlach, 2015; Vaughan & Rodriguez, 2014; Worth & Smith, 2017).

In contrast, critical social psychology is heavily influenced by emancipatory and social justice ideals. These ideals value bringing forth the perspective of minority groups to create positive and affirming changes in the lives of marginalised individuals (Worth & Smith, 2017). It places considerable emphasis on exploring environmental characteristics uniquely experienced by under-explored minority groups –

such as historical, legal, organisational and social contexts (Worst & Smith, 2017). A key focus of this approach is to identify the unmet needs of diverse populations and the development of specific supports to meet those needs (Worst & Smith, 2017); similar to sociological LGBTQ+ Family Functioning and LGBTQ+ Parents in Schools Studies (McNair & Perlesz, 2004; Rawsthorne, 2009). Endorsed methodologies within this disciplinary approach include the use of 'scientific' quantitative measures to explore how frequent a given factor may be present in the environment; *as well as* qualitative methods to privilege and explore the perceptions, experiences or behaviours of individuals (Worth & Smith, 2017).

Similar to critical psychology, positive psychology (or strength-based psychology) rejects the deficit or medicalised views often adopted in traditional psychology. It instead endorses the exploration of environmental characteristics on an individual's development (Vaughan & Rodriguez, 2014). Strength-based psychology particularly focusses on exploring the potential protective role social organisations (such as schools) can play in an individual's development as a means to overcome (and potentially offer solutions to) challenges identified in over-represented deficit models of research (Vaughan & Rodriguez, 2014). This framing may be particularly useful in exploring LGBTQ+ parents in schools with its focus on exploring positive aspects of organisations that aim to improve the strength-based outcomes (for example, perceived support and well-being) for the individuals they serve (Vaughan & Rodriguez, 2014). Endorsed methodological considerations within positive psychology in LGBTQ+ research include:

- research designs inclusive of LGBTQ+ identities,
- utilisation of quantitative and qualitative mixed methodologies, and
- a focus on supportive experiences within social organisations (Vaughan et al., 2014).

In keeping with critical social psychology's privileging of an interdisciplinary approach, the new Australian study this book reports on therefore utilised Urie Bronfenbrenner's psycho-sociological Theory of Ecological Development (Bronfenbrenner & Crouter, 1983) as a theoretical framework. This theory offers opportunities to explore LGBTQ+ parents' positive experiences in school contexts and their perspectives on commonly endorsed inclusive practices – as detailed in the next section.

3.4 Bronfenbrenner's theory of ecological development

This section of the chapter introduces Urie Bronfenbrenner and his Theory of Ecological Development as a useful tool to explore LGBTQ+ parents' experiences, within a holistic framing. A sub-section providing an introduction to the theory is followed with several sections showing an application of the framework via the Australian real-world case study.

3.4.1 Urie Bronfenbrenner and his theory of ecological development

Urie Bronfenbrenner (1917–2005) was a developmental psychologist with a focus on human development and social policy. He believed that liberal and conservative psychological approaches (such as those considering cognitive development, gender role behaviours, and educational outcomes in Child Development Studies 1970s+) failed to account for environmental characteristics that could influence the development of an individual (Bronfenbrenner & Crouter, 1983). He believed firmly in the advancement of social policies that adopted a holistic investigation of an individual's development including psychological characteristics (found in conservative and liberal psychologies) alongside an analysis of environmental factors and contexts that may be influential to the developing individual. His research model also offers an adaptable theoretical lens that may holistically integrate previous inter-disciplinary research related to LGBTQ+ parented family functioning and experiences within school research into a concise framework.

The Theory of Ecological Development has developed over 30 years (Bronfenbrenner, 1974; Bronfenbrenner, 1999; Bronfenbrenner & Crouter, 1983). It is an extension of traditional nature vs. nurture theories in developmental psychology (Piaget, 1969; Vygotsky, 1978). This theory aims to integrate theories of individual development (e.g. Piaget's developmental stages for the individual) with environmental theories of development (e.g. Vygotsky's socio-cultural development accounts). The Theory of Ecological Development offers several potential strengths to exploring the experiences of LGBTQ+ parented families in school contexts, including its ability to:

* avoid potential biases or heteronormative assumptions implicit in some alternate theories of development (Allen & Demo, 1995);
* proactively and practically inform the development of school policies, practices and procedures inclusive of identified minority groups (Burns, 2011);

- offer researchers and policy developers a comprehensive theory of development that accommodates the inter-disciplinary development of LGBTQ+ parent research and its many facets (e.g. Parent in school research see Liang & Cohrssen, 2020; and International legal settings see Siegel et al., 2021);
- offer researchers and policy developers a flexible and adaptive theoretical framework that has been applied to previous LGBTQ+ parents within school studies (Goldberg, Black, Sweeney, et al., 2017; Goldberg & Smith, 2014a, 2014b; Herbstrith & Busse, 2020);
- align with models advocated by international educational authorities as a method to explore the school experiences of diverse sexual orientation and gender diversity minority groups (UNESCO, 2016); and
- potentially address previous general critiques of LGBTQ+ parent research including the lack of theoretical frameworks and appropriate methodologies used in the field which may limit the development of this body of research (Farr et al., 2017).

The Theory of Ecological Development (Bronfenbrenner & Crouter, 1983) states that individuals develop embedded within five overarching systems. These systems include; the Individual (and all of their characteristics), the Microsystem, the Mesosystem, the Exosystem, the Macrosystem and the Chronosystem (see Figure 3.1).

At the centre of Ecological Theory is *the Individual*. Theoretically, the individual is an acknowledgement and inclusion of conservative (e.g. national census data) and liberal (e.g. Child Development Studies in the 1970s+) psychological approaches that focus on identifying different aspects of individuals and their developmental outcomes. The individual is also placed at the centre of the framework to highlight the various levels of any given context that can potentially influence how an individual behaves, and thus their individual development. For example, while LGBTQ+ parents are at their child's school their behaviours are governed by external environmental governances simultaneously. These environmental factors can include things like national laws, socio-cultural norms of acceptable behaviour, school policies and procedures, and interpersonal interactions with others (e.g. teachers or other parents) in fixed locations (e.g. on school grounds, in the family home, or in the classroom).

Practically, the Individual includes demographic and development characteristics of an individual including their age, sex, relationship status, cognitive development, gender identity, education, socio-economic status, race or ethnicity, personal attitudes and beliefs,

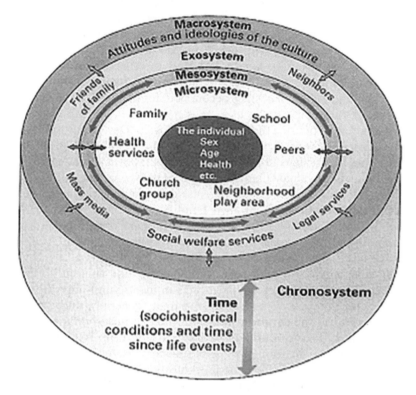

Figure 3.1 Bronfenbrenner's Theory of Ecological Development (1974, p. 47).

health etc. Various aspects or characteristics of the individual (such as age, race or identification as LGBTQ+) may be related to different experiences in the environment and different developmental outcomes. For example, the choices, opportunities and responsibilities of adults differ significantly from that of children.

The *Microsystem* includes institutional and social contexts individuals repeatedly interact with during their lifespan. The more frequently and repeatedly individuals interact with a given environment, the more influential it may be on an individual's development. In the case of parents, this may include regular activities to maintain families such as maintaining their child's school enrolment, attendance at religious or community organisations and consultation with family health services.

The *Mesosystem* includes the influence of at least two settings in the development of the individual, such as work, religious communities and school contexts. The *Exosystem* includes settings and contexts that individuals have less control over and indirectly influence personal development. These include social factors such as mass media, legal services and less frequented social contexts such as local community events and friends of the family. The *Macrosystem* includes broad social attitudes, laws and ideologies of the culture in which an individual develops and the *Chronosystem* accommodates time and the changing nature of these contexts.

The strength of using the Theory of Ecological Development (Bronfenbrenner & Crouter, 1983) as a theoretical framework is its ability to synthesise previous research and gain greater insight into environmental and individual characteristics of LGBTQ+ parented families. Information about LGBTQ+ parents' demographic characteristics (e.g. income and education), their families (e.g. pathways to parenthood, family formation), their experiences in social organisations (e.g. schools) and their experiences of larger systems (e.g. anti-LGBTQ+ mass-media) contribute to gaining insightful details around the lives and experiences of their families. This information is useful for researchers, policy makers and advocates in identifying supports and challenges experienced by LGBTQ+ parents generally, and can be used to inform the development of holistic and inclusive supportive policies (Goodrich & Luke, 2009; Liang & Cohrssen, 2020; Ryan & Martin, 2000). This framework is particularly useful in offering in-depth insight into specific national contexts, given the highly differential global treatment and protections offered to LGBTQ+ identities.

The first chapter of the book showed international legislative contexts for LGBTQ+ parents vary. Countries around the world also differ widely in terms of the dominant social attitudes, and protections offered to LGBTQ+ identities and families varying from affirmative to criminalised framings (Perales et al., 2019; Siegel et al., 2021). These societal framings in the Macrosystem can have multiple influences on the development of LGBTQ+ parents and families including their intentions to seek parenthood, access to assisted reproductive technologies, representations in mass media, financial protections, recognition and acknowledgement in social organisations (e.g. schools), to name a few areas (Gato et al., 2019; Hill et al., 2020; Perales et al., 2019; Shenkman & Abramovitch, 2020; Siegel et al., 2021; Tate & Patterson, 2019). Given the highly discrepant treatment and acknowledgement of LGBTQ+ identities globally, there is a need to explore national settings individually recognising the cultural, societal and legal norms and contexts which differ from nation to nation. The next section highlights Bronfenbrenner's Theory of Ecological Development relevant to LGBTQ+ parented families in Australia as an exemplary case study.

3.4.2 Bronfenbrenner's theory of ecological development in practice: an Australian case study

Research on LGBTQ+ parented families offer insights into various aspects of their lives, including pathways to parenthood, experiences in social institutions (such as schools and family health), social supports (such as relationships with LGBTQ+ communities and family of origin), and mass-media. However, these studies have developed from a range of different international contexts which may make it difficult to compare and contrast or transfer findings given the differences in national socio-cultural views and legislative protections offered to LGBTQ+ parents (Perales et al., 2019; Siegel et al., 2021). As a result, it becomes important to report Australian research that has explored various facets of parents' experiences, inherently including the socio-cultural and legislative contexts in which parents develop.

Australian research exploring LGBTQ+ parented families has developed from various sources. To date research with the largest sample sizes in Australia is drawn from incidental national census data (Australian Bureau of Statistics/ABS, 2016) partnerships between NGOs and researchers (Hill et al., 2020) and research teams (Perlesz et al., 2010). The contributions of this research have highlighted LGBTQ+ parents are unique in various ways, including demographic characteristics, family formation practices, and their experiences in social contexts such as schools and family health care. The following section highlights various important dimensions and experiences of Australian LGBTQ+ parents to create an exemplary 'snap-shot' of relevant information for public service organisations, policy developers and educational professionals.

3.4.3 The individual – LGBTQ+ parents' characteristics

Research exploring the *Individual* – the LGBTQ+ parent – to date in Australia have explored demographic characteristics, pathways to parenthood and child development characteristics. The largest samples currently within research are drawn from the Work Play Love Study (Perlesz et al., 2010; Power et al., 2010, 2012), The Australian Bureau of Statistics (ABS, 2016) and the Private Lives 3 Study (Hill et al., 2020). Current national census data indicate that same-sex couples have increased by 39% and same-sex parented families have increased from 12% to 15% from 2011 to 2016, parenting around 10,500 children (ABS, 2016). Although these numbers are potentially underrepresented – only identifying co-parents who reside in the same household and those parents who choose to disclose information about their family formations (ABS, 2016).

Australian LGBTQ+ parented families have been consistently found to have higher levels of education and income compared to national samples (ABS, 2016; Crouch et al., 2014; Hill et al., 2020; Perlesz et al., 2010; Power et al., 2012). There are ongoing arguments as to whether this is a characteristic of LGBTQ+ adults generally, a by-product of parents utilising costly Assisted Reproductive Technologies (e.g. insemination clinics and IVF), private surrogacy arrangements or merely characteristics of those who participate in research (Crouch et al., 2014; Power et al., 2010).

In terms of pathways to parenthood, the methods of gaining parental status are diverse. Although the majority of LGBTQ+ parents in Australia gain parenthood through sexual intercourse in previous heterosexual relationships, a growing number of parents are gaining parenthood in same-sex partnerships (Crouch et al., 2014; Hill et al., 2020; Power et al., 2010, 2012). Potential methods to seeking parenthood in single or same-sex couples include biological materials donated from known and unknown donors, assisted reproductive technologies (e.g. IVF, insemination clinics), surrogacy arrangements as well as foster and adoptions arrangements (Crouch et al., 2014; Hill et al., 2020; Power et al., 2010, 2012). Researchers have also noted that Australian LGBTQ+ parents may privilege pathways to parenthood that include biological relatedness to children (e.g. surrogacy or donor arrangements) compared to parents in international contexts (Dempsey, 2013).

3.4.4 Microsystems – LGBTQ+ parents' frequent contexts

Microsystems are contexts which individuals frequently and repetitively engaged with, which are argued to have a direct influence on the development of individuals (Bronfenbrenner & Crouter, 1983). Microsystem settings particularly explored by Australian research include child development studies, LGBTQ+ parent family structures and relationships, and their navigations in frequented public service organisations including schools and family health services.

3.4.4.1 Families

Australian studies exploring the developmental outcomes of children parented by LGBTQ+ parents have noted, similar to previous international research (Tasker, 2005), that the sexual orientation and gender identity/expression of parents has little influence on various developmental outcomes or characteristics of children (Crouch et al., 2014). Compared to national samples, LGBTQ+ parented children do not differ in terms of physical health, emotional and behavioural well-being, quality of relationships with parents and social behaviours (Crouch et al., 2014). However, perceived stigma was negatively related to children's mental health and well being, and family functioning generally (Crouch et al., 2014). This warrants further investigation into the experiences of LGBTQ+ parents in settings such as family health and school contexts where stigmatising and discriminatory events have been noted as particularly challenging (Crouch et al., 2014).

Family structures and relationships have been the main focus of parent research as a means to inform public service professionals and policy makers of the diversity and support inherent in LGBTQ+ parented families (McNair & Perlesz, 2004; Power et al., 2010). Research of this type has particularly explored the parenting structures of LGBTQ+ parented families, the division of work and domestic labour, and parents' relationships with families of origin (or grandparents). In terms of parenting structures, LGBTQ+ parented families in Australia are notably diverse. Although it has been noted that the majority of LGBTQ+ families adhere to traditional dual-gendered families in having two primary carers of children in committed relationships, studies show LGBTQ+ parents may also include single parents or family formations that include more than two active adults in parent-like roles of children (Power et al., 2010). Noted family formations can include couples in current relationships, parenting with known donor involvement, co-parenting with ex heterosexual partners, co-parenting with ex-same sex partners, multiple parental roles where more than two parents are active parental caregivers (including gay fathers, lesbian mothers and their corresponding partners), the inclusion of donors or surrogates as active caretakers, as well as step or blended family constellations (Dempsey, 2010; Perlesz & McNair, 2004; Perlesz et al., 2010; Power et al., 2012). LGBTQ+ families can also acknowledge close friends of the family (known as 'family of choice') as aunts or uncles, that may be responsible for caregiving roles of children and defy assumptions that family members are based on strict bio-legal definitions (Perlesz et al., 2006; McNair & Perlesz, 2004).

Lesbian parented families have been noted to be more egalitarian in sharing work and household/carer roles compared to heterosexual parented families (Perlesz et al., 2010). Gay parented families have been noted to replicate traditional domestic-work divisions of labour where one parent may have more caregiving responsibilities for the child than another (Power et al., 2012). Contrary to assumptions of normative parent-child relationships, the primary carer of young children may not always be the parent biologically linked to the child (Perlesz et al., 2010). In terms of the number of children, LGBTQ+ parents have been noted to be more likely to have one child compared to national samples (ABS, 2016), although can consist of one to three or more children (Crouch et al., 2014; Hill et al., 2020; Perlesz et al., 2010).

In terms of family of origin, research appears to be somewhat mixed in whether LGBTQ+ parents enjoy support from their parents (or grandparents). Relationships with parents can vary from supportive quality relationships (McNair & Perlesz, 2004), to less supportive types (Perales et al., 2019; Riggs et al., 2016; von Doussa et al., 2015). In some cases, acquiring parenthood builds closer ties with parents of origin where the primary identity of parents shifts from being an LGBTQ+ son or daughter to the mother or father of a grandchild (Power et al., 2012). Noted family characteristics with less support from families of origin have been related to children conceived in ex-heterosexual relationships as well as religious, cultural and linguistic diverse families (Perales et al., 2019; Power et al., 2012). In cases of parents having weak support from families of origin, researchers have argued the need for formal organisations (such as schools) to connect parents to other potential informal sources of support such as local or LGBTQ+ related community groups (Rawsthorne, 2009).

3.4.4.2 *LGBTQ+ community*

A small body of research has explored parents' perceived support and connection to LGBTQ+ community groups. Similar to support from the family of origin, this research has noted parents can differ in their connection to LGBTQ+ community groups (Ruth McNair et al., 2002; Perlesz & McNair, 2004), despite such community connections being related to beneficial outcomes in individuals perceived support and well-being (Hill et al., 2020). In cases where parents may lack support from families of origin and the LGBTQ+ community, researchers have argued the need for formal organisations such as schools and family health services to act as points of referral to other forms of informal supports such as local LGBTQ+ community or parenting groups (McNair & Perlesz, 2004; Rawsthorne, 2009).

3.4.4.3 *Social organisations*

Research exploring the experiences of LGBTQ+ parents navigating social organisations such as family health services (Mcnair et al., 2008) and school environments (Lindsay et al., 2006) appear to highlight similar challenges for parents. Noted challenges in these organisations typically include cases where social organisations lack LGBTQ+ inclusive policies, and lack procedures and practices that accommodate non-heterosexual and non-cis gendered family constellations (Cloughessy et al., 2018, 2019; Lindsay et al., 2006; Mcnair et al., 2008; McNair & Perlesz, 2004; Mikhailovich et al., 2001; Shields et al., 2012; Skattebol & Ferfolja, 2007). Certain features of Microsystems (such as schools and family health) may prove particularly problematic for LGBTQ+ parented families. These include official forms that assume families consist of parents biologically or legally related to children, use of gendered language in documents such as 'Mother' and 'Father' that can exclude LGBTQ+ forms of family diversity, policies and procedures that assume parents and guardians have legal custodianship or biological relations to children, assumptions that families consist of up to two adults in parental roles and lack of knowledge or negative stereotypical beliefs in public service professionals regarding LGBTQ+ forms of family diversity (Cloughessy et al., 2018, 2019; Lindsay et al., 2006; Mcnair et al., 2008; Mikhailovich et al., 2001; Shields et al., 2012).

Social organisations that consist of such exclusionary practices which assume all service consumers are heterosexual or cis-gendered have been related to a range of negative outcomes for parents. These outcomes include anxiety around the legal recognition and rights of non-genetically related parents, confusion and concern over 'how much' personal information about family constellations to disclose in forms, inappropriate and discriminatory questioning around family structures and pathways to parenthood, and frustrations around having to repeatedly 'come out' and educate service professionals around LGBTQ+ forms of family diversity (Mcnair et al., 2008; McNair & Perlesz, 2004; Mikhailovich et al., 2001; Shields et al., 2012; Skattebol & Ferfolja, 2007). In recognition of these challenges, researchers tend to advocate for (though have not directly researched the desire for) similar LGBTQ+ related supportive features in social organisations to create more welcoming environments. These support features include non-gendered and inclusive forms and documents, training in-service professionals around LGBTQ+ forms of family diversity, explicit inclusion of LBGTQ+ parents within organisational policies and materials or artefacts (e.g. books, posters) that reflect LGBTQ+ parents and their families (Cloughessy et al., 2018, 2019; Lindsay et al., 2006; Mcnair et al., 2008). Additionally, researchers have argued the need for collaboration with representatives of the LGBTQ+ parent community to ensure the development of appropriately sensitive and inclusive policies and procedures (Mcnair et al., 2008).

3.4.5   Exosystems – LGBTQ+ parents' broader environments

Exosystem contexts include environments that individuals have less control over and may indirectly influence an individuals' development. These include social factors such as mass media, social welfare systems, legal services and neighbourhoods. Research exploring Australian mass media depictions of LGBTQ+ identities have highlighted various ways the media can pose unique challenging experiences for LGBTQ+ generally, and specifically in educational contexts.

3.4.5.1   Mass media

LGBTQ+ identities have repeatedly featured as a heatedly debated topic in Australian mass media as discussed in the first chapter of the book, particularly in regard to proposed legislative amendments (e.g. same-sex marriage) and 'if and how' LGBTQ+ identities should be represented or protected within educational contexts (Ferfolja & Ullman, 2017; Law, 2017). Media events that have particularly brought high focus to date have included the recent same-sex marriage (or marriage equality) postal survey in 2017, the LGBTQ+ inclusive Safe Schools Coalition in 2016 and the religious freedom debate around a range of bill proposals at federal and state levels that have been ongoing since 2018. Recent debates particularly relevant to LGBTQ+ parents that have been especially vicious in their construction of LGBTQ+ people included the same-sex marriage debate, and arguments over funding of the Safe Schools Coalition (an initially Victorian-based programme that became national raised much furore over perceptions that LGBTQ+ information was harmful to youth, to be ultimately defunded or closed in all locations except Victoria in recent years).

3.4.5.2   Safe schools coalition

From 2013 to 2016 the Australian government supported development and implementation of a voluntary anti-bullying LGBTQ+ inclusive school curriculum program (Law, 2017). The United Nations highlighted the project as a particularly strong example of how schools could create inclusive and welcoming school environments for people who may identify as LGBTQ+ (UNESCO, 2016). However, the program received a high level of backlash from concerned media, government officials and religious bodies for introducing inappropriate material to young people (Law, 2017) – despite a rather tame anti-bullying focus based mostly on suicide reduction research around

LGBTQ+ youth (Hillier et al., 2010; Jones, 2015). Negative perceptions of the project identified in public and media debates included the potential perversion or corruption of innocent youth, concerns around distorting gender norms in students, infringements against the rights of parents and the marginalisation of cis-gendered heterosexual school community members (Ferfolja & Ullman, 2017; Thompson, 2019).

Discourses in the media at the time generally positioned LGBTQ+ identities and LGBTQ+ inclusive classrooms as risky topics to discuss in school contexts with arguments such as school content may cause students to be confused in their gender roles and sexual orientations (Ferfolja & Ullman, 2017; Thompson, 2019). As a result, Australian schools may deem LGBTQ+ inclusive school programs dangerous and risky endeavours to include in school classrooms with the realistic potential for political and local community backlash when targeted specifically for attack by Murdoch Media (Law, 2017). This is despite the repetitive recommendation in LGBTQ+ parent-school research for schools to incorporate materials and learning activities inclusive of LGBTQ+ parents and families as a means to create welcoming school environments, and address marginalising and exclusionary experiences noted in school contexts (Bartholomaeus & Riggs, 2017; Cloughessy et al., 2019; Lindsay et al., 2006). Further, the program promoted the enumerated policy protection of LGBTQ+ students against bullying based on Australian research which showed this contributed to contexts in which suicide rates and violence were significantly reduced (Hillier et al., 2010; Jones, 2015).

3.4.5.3 Same-sex marriage debate (marriage equality)

In 2017 the Australian government authorised the same-sex marriage (or marriage equality) plebiscite. This involved a nationwide postal survey where Australian citizens of voting age were required to indicate their support for same-sex marriage. As part of this process, two peak organised groups representing the Yes and No votes created and distributed a wide range of mass media, social media and print media coverage to build awareness and support for their campaigns (ABS, 2017). Between the 9th of August and 15th of November 15,574 media items were distributed which reached a cumulative audience of over 427 million (ABS, 2017). The Yes vote campaign tended to focus on topics of social justice, equality and recognition of LGBTQ+ families as another form of diversity while the No vote was noted to perpetuate 'common sense' beliefs, inaccuracies and misrepresentations about gender identity and sexuality (Knight et al., 2017), similar to negative beliefs iterated in anti-LGBTQ+ research in 1990s+. A small body of research emerged in response to the potential impact this nationwide event may have on the health and well-being of the LG-BTQ+ community. This research found that exposure to the 'No' campaign material (which typically included discriminatory messages in the media) caused negative mental health outcomes and psychological distress in adults who identified as LGBTQ+ (Bartos et al., 2021; Hill et al., 2020; Verrelli et al., 2019). In recognition of the ongoing heated national debates regarding the rights and protections of LGBTQ+ individuals, and the potential for such supports to negatively influence family health and well-being (Crouch et al., 2014), researchers have argued the need for public service professionals and public policy to be mindful and inclusive of the unique challenges experienced and supports required for adults and parents who may identify as LGBTQ+ (Bartos et al., 2021; Knight et al., 2017).

3.4.6 Macrosystems – national ideologies, attitudes & beliefs impacting LGBTQ+ parents

The *Macrosystem* includes dominant ideologies, attitudes and beliefs prevalent within a national context, including national laws. In 2017 79.5% of voting-aged Australians took part in a national survey indicating their support or opposition for the legalisation of same-sex marriage, or marriage equality (ABS, 2017). The results indicated that 38.4% of voters opposed marriage equality while 61.6% supported the legislative amendment, which was formally acknowledged in legislation in 2017 (ABS, 2017). This indicates that although the majority of Australians support the potential for LGBTQ+ parents and families, there is an evident split in societal views toward LGBTQ+ identities, couples and parents with close to 40% of the population not supporting the legislative amendment. Research exploring individual characteristics related to less positive views of LGBTQ+ parents and families include individual beliefs regarding appropriate gender norms and gender role modelling (Webb et al., 2020), similar to media discourses concerning the Safe Schools Coalition, marriage equality and anti-LGBTQ+ research in the 1990s+.

3.5 Summary of key points

Researchers have argued that educational organisations need to adopt a holistic approach to developing inclusive and progressive public policy to accommodate the unique needs of LGBTQ+ parents (Liang & Cohrssen, 2020; McNair et al., 2002; Rawsthorne, 2009). This includes taking note of potential challenging and protective factors parents experience in a variety of contexts that are related to family health and well-being; including informal and formal social supports, experiences in public service organisations and larger social factors such as highly publicised political debates (Knight et al., 2017; Rawsthorne, 2009).

This case study has attempted to inform inclusive policy development and public service professionals about the diversity in LGBTQ+ parented families, and common challenges and protective factors identified within previous Australian research. A brief summary of each 'layer' of the ecological system, and demographic characteristics of individuals, are highlighted below:

- Individual characteristics – LGBTQ+ parents:
  - are increasingly common in Australia, seeking parenthood in various ways.
  - do not differ from cis/heterosexual parented families in raising well-adjusted healthy children.
- Microsystem characteristics – LGBTQ+ parented families:
  - differ in their structures, support from extended families and LGBTQ+ community (including chosen families).
  - find social organisation policies, practices, procedures and professionals that do not include, acknowledge or represent them particularly challenging.
- Exosystem characteristics – LGBTQ+ parent communities:
  - experience negative health and well-being outcomes around mass media and public 'moral panics' related to 'if and how' they should be acknowledged, protected and recognised within social organisations and society.
  - have unique needs and suffer due to biases social organisations (e.g. schools and public health providers) should be mindful in policy development.
- Macrosystem Characteristics – the concept of LGBTQ+ parents:
  - are increasingly affirmed within greater acknowledgement and protections in national laws and Australian attitudes.
  - nonetheless may only be supported by around two-thirds of the public given marriage equality legislative amendment voting; 38.6% were opposed, and a range of views are held by Australians on related laws and issues.

3.6 Conclusion & next chapter

This chapter justified the use of critical social psychology, strength-based psychology and the Theory of Ecological Development as a culturally sensitive lens – showing Bronfenbrenner's Theory of Ecological Development can develop a 'holistic snapshot' of various environmental contexts influential in the lives of parents using Australia as an exemplary case study. The next chapter highlights the study's application of the theory, research questions and methodology, and the characteristics of Individuals (participant demographics) and Microsystems (school environments) uncovered.

References

ABS. (2016). *2071.0- Census of Population and Housing: Reflecting Australia, 2016*. Retrieved from https://www.abs.gov.au/ausstats/abs@.nsf/Lookup/2071.0main+features852016

ABS. (2017). *1800.0- Australian Marriage Law Postal Survey, 2017*. Retrieved from https://www.abs.gov.au/websitedbs/D3310114.nsf/home/AMLPS+-+Privacy+Policy

Allen, K. R., & Demo, D. H. (1995). The families of lesbians and gay men. *Journal of Marriage and Family, 57*, 111–127.

Anderssen, N., Amlie, C., & Ytterøy, E. A. (2002). Outcomes for children with lesbian or gay parents. *Scandinavian Journal of Psychology, 43*(4), 335–351.

Bartholomaeus, C., & Riggs, D. W. (2017). Whole-of-school approaches to supporting transgender students, staff, and parents. *The International Journal of Transgenderism, 18*(4), 361–366.

Bartos, S. E., Noon, D. W., & Frost, D. M. (2021). Minority stress, campaign messages and political participation during the Australian marriage plebiscite. *Sexuality Research and Social Policy, 18*(1), 75–86.

Bliss, G. K., & Harris, M. B. (1998). Experiences of Gay and Lesbian Teachers and Parents with Coming Out in a School Setting. *Journal of Gay & Lesbian Social Services, 8*(2), 13–28.

Bronfenbrenner, U. (1974). Developmental research, public policy, and the ecology of childhood. *Child Development, 45*(1), 1–5.

Bronfenbrenner, U., & Crouter, A. (1983). The evolution of environmental models in developmental research. In P. Mussen & W. Kessen (Eds.), *Handbook of Child Psychology Volume 1* (pp. 357–414). New York: John Wiley.

Bronfenbrenner, U. (1999). Environments in developmental perspective: Theoretical and operational models. In S. L. Friedman & T. D. Wachs (Eds.), *Measuring environments across the lifespan: Emerging methods and concepts* (pp. 3–28). Washington, DC: American Psychological Association.

Burns, M. (2011). School psychology research. *School Psychology Review, 40*(1), 132–139.

Casper, V., Schultz, S., & Wickens, E. (1992). Breaking the silences. *Teachers College Record, 94*(1), 109–137.

Cloughessy, K, & Waniganayake, M. (2015). Raised eyebrows. *Children & Society, 29*(5), 377–387.

Cloughessy, K., Waniganayake, M., & Blatterer, H. (2018). This is our family. We do not hide who we are. *Journal of GLBT Family Studies, 14*(4), 381–399.

Cloughessy, K., Waniganayake, M., & Blatterer, H. (2019). The good and the bad. *Journal of Research in Childhood Education, 33*(3), 446–458.

Crouch, S. R., Waters, E., McNair, R., Power, J., & Davis, E. (2014). Parent-reported measures of child health and wellbeing in same-sex parent families. *BMC Public Health, 14*(1), 635–635.

DeLamatar, J., Myers, D., & Collett, J. (2015). *Social Psychology* (Vol. 8). Taylor and Francis. Retrieved from https://ebookcentral-proquest-com. simsrad.net.ocs.mq.edu.au/lib/mqu/detail.action?docID=1652845#

Dempsey, D. (2010). Conceiving and negotiating reproductive relationships. *Sociology, 44*(6), 1145–1162.

Dempsey, D. (2013). Same-sex parented families in Australia. *Australian Institute of Family Studies (18)*, 1–26. Retrieved from: https://aifs.gov.au/cfca/publications/same-sex-parented-families-australia

Farr, R. H., Tasker, F., & Goldberg, A. E. (2017). Theory in highly cited studies of sexual minority parent families. *Journal of Homosexuality, 64*(9), 1143–1179.

Ferfolja, T., & Ullman, J. (2017). Gender and sexuality in education and health. *Sex Education, 17*(3), 235–241.

Gabb, J. (2005). Locating lesbian parent families. *Gender, Place and Culture, 12*(4), 419–432.

Gahan, L. (2018). Separated same-sex parents. *Sociological Research Online, 23*(1), 245–261.

Gato, J., Leal, D., & Tasker, F. (2019). Parenting desires, parenting intentions, and anticipation of stigma upon parenthood among lesbian, bisexual, and heterosexual women in Portugal. *Journal of Lesbian Studies, 23*(4), 451–463.

Goldberg, A. E., Black, K., Sweeney, K., & Moyer, A. (2017). Lesbian, gay, and heterosexual adoptive parents' perceptions of inclusivity and receptiveness in early childhood education settings. *Journal of Research in Childhood Education, 31*(1), 141–159.

Goldberg, A. E., & Smith, J. Z. (2014a). Perceptions of stigma and self-reported school engagement in same-sex couples with young children. *Psychology of Sexual Orientation and Gender Diversity, 1*(3), 202–212. https://doi.org/10.1037/sgd0000052

Goldberg, A. E., & Smith, J. Z. (2014b). Preschool selection considerations and experiences of school mistreatment among lesbian, gay, and heterosexual adoptive parents. *Early Childhood Research Quarterly, 29*(1), 64–75.

Gonsiorek, J. (1982). An Introduction to Mental Health Issues and Homosexuality. *The American Behavioral Scientist, 25*(4), 367–384.

Goodrich, K. M., & Luke, M. (2009). LGBTQ responsive school counseling. *Journal of LGBT Issues in Counseling, 3*(2), 113–127.

Gray, E., Harris, A., & Jones, T. (2016). Australian LGBTQ teachers, exclusionary spaces and points of interruption. *Sexualities, 19*(3), 286–303.

Gundlach, H. (2015). Critical Psychology. In N. Smelser & P. Baltes (Eds.), *International Encyclopedia of the Social & Behavioural Sciences* (pp. 261–265). Wurzburg: Pergamon.

Herbstrith, J. C., & Busse, G. A. (2020). Seven million and counting. *Journal of Educational and Psychological Consultation, 30*(1), 29–62.

Hill, A. O., Bourne, A., McNair, R., Carman, M., & Lyons, A. (2020). *Private Lives 3.* Melbourne: ARCSHS.

Hillier, L., Jones, T., Monagle, M., Overton, N., Gahan, L., Blackman, J., & Mitchell, A. (2010). *Writing Themselves In 3.* Melbourne: ARCSHS.

Jones, T. (2015). *Policy and Gay, Lesbian, Bisexual, Transgender and Intersex Students.* New York: Springer.

Knight, K. W., Stephenson, S. E., West, S., Delatycki, M. B., Jones, C. A., Little, M. H., Patton, G. C., Sawyer, S. M., Skinner, S. R., Telfer, M. M., Wake, M., North, K. N., & Oberklaid, F. (2017). The kids are OK. *Medical Journal of Australia, 207*(9), 374–375.

Lambert, S. (2005). Gay and lesbian families. *The Family Journal, 13*(1), 43–51.

Law, B. (2017). Moral panic 101. *Quarterly Essay, 67,* 1–80.

Liang, X., & Cohrssen, C. (2020). Towards creating inclusive environments for LGBTIQ-parented families in early childhood education and care settings. *Australasian Journal of Early Childhood, 45*(1), 43–55.

Lindsay, J., Perlesz, A., Brown, R., McNair, R., De Vaus, D., & Pitts, M. (2006). Stigma or respect. *Sociology, 40*(6), 1059–1077.

Mcnair, R., Brown, R., Perlesz, A., Lindsay, J., De Vaus, D., & Pitts, M. (2008). Lesbian parents negotiating the health care system in Australia. *Health Care for Women International, 29*(2), 91–114.

McNair, R., Dempsey, D., Wise, S., & Perlesz, A. (2002). Lesbian parenting. *Family Matters, 63,* 40–49.

McNair, R., & Perlesz, A. (2004). Lesbian parenting. *Australian and New Zealand Journal of Family Therapy, 25*(3), 129–140.

Mikhailovich, K., Martin, S., & Lawton, S. (2001). Lesbian and gay parents. *International Journal of Sexuality and Gender Studies, 6*(3), 181–191.

Perales, F., Simpson Reeves, L., Plage, S., & Baxter, J. (2019). The family lives of Australian lesbian, gay and bisexual people. *Sexuality Research & Social Policy, 17*(1), 43–60.

Perlesz, A., Brown, R., Lindsay, J., McNair, R., De Vaus, D., & Pitts, M. (2006). Family in transition. *Journal of Family Therapy, 28*(2), 175–199.

Perlesz, A., & McNair, R. (2004). Lesbian parenting. *Australian and New Zealand Journal of Family Therapy, 25*(3), 129–140.

Perlesz, A., Power, J., Brown, R., McNair, R., Schofield, M., Pitts, M., Barrett, A., & Bickerdike, A. (2010). Organising work and home in same-sex parented families. *Australian and New Zealand Journal of Family Therapy, 31*(4), 374–391.

Piaget, J. (1969). *Science of education and the psychology of the child.* New York: Viking.

Power, J., Perlesz, A., Brown, R., Schofield, M., Pitts, M., McNair, R., & Bickerdike, A. (2010). Diversity, tradition and family. *Gay and Lesbian Issues and Psychology Review, 6*(2), 66.

Power, J., Perlesz, A., Mcnair, R., Schofield, M., Pitts, M., Brown, R., & Bickerdike, A. (2012). Gay and bisexual dads and diversity. *Journal of Family Studies, 18*(2–3), 143–154.

Power, J. J., Perlesz, A., Schofield, M. J., Pitts, M. K., Brown, R., McNair, R., Barrett, A., & Bickerdike, A. (2010). Understanding resilience in same-sex parented families. *BMC Public Health, 10*(1), 115–115.

Rawsthorne, M. L. (2009). Just like other families? *Australian Social Work, 62*(1), 45–60.

Riggs, D. W., Power, J., & von Doussa, H. (2016). Parenting and Australian trans and gender diverse people. *The International Journal of Transgenderism, 17*(2), 59–65.

Ryan, D., & Martin, A. (2000). Lesbian, gay, bisexual, and transgender parents in the school systems. *School Psychology Review, 29*(2), 207–216.

Shenkman, G., & Abramovitch, M. (2020). Estimated likelihood of parenthood and its association with psychological well-being among sexual minorities and heterosexual counterparts. *Sexuality Research and Social Policy, 18*(2), 1–12.

Shields, L., Zappia, T., Blackwood, D., Watkins, R., Wardrop, J., & Chapman, R. (2012). Lesbian, gay, bisexual, and transgender parents seeking health care for their children. *Worldviews on Evidence-Based Nursing, 9*(4), 200–209.

Siegel, M., Assenmacher, C., Meuwly, N., & Zemp, M. (2021). The legal vulnerability model for same-sex parent families. *Frontiers in Psychology, 12*, 644258.

Skattebol, J., & Ferfolja, T. (2007). Voices from an enclave. *Australasian Journal of Early Childhood, 32*(1), 10–18.

Tasker, F. (2005). Lesbian mothers, gay fathers, and their children. *Journal of Developmental and Behavioral Pediatrics, 26*(3), 224–240.

Tate, D. P., & Patterson, C. J. (2019). Desire for parenthood in context of other life aspirations among lesbian, gay, and heterosexual young adults. *Frontiers in Psychology, 10*, 2679.

Thompson, J. D. (2019). Predatory schools and student non-lives. *Sex Education, 19*(1), 41–53.

UNESCO. (2016). *Out In The Open: Education Sector Responses to Violence Based on Sexual Orientation and Gender Identity/Expression.* Paris: UNESCO.

Vaughan, M. D., & Rodriguez, E. M. (2014). LGBT strengths. *Psychology of Sexual Orientation and Gender Diversity, 1*(4), 325–334.

Vaughan, M. D., Miles, J., Parent, M. C., Lee, H. S., Tilghman, J. D., & Prokhorets, S. (2014). A content analysis of LGBT-Themed positive psychology articles. *Psychology of Sexual Orientation and Gender Diversity, 1*(4), 313–324.

Verrelli, S., White, F. A., Harvey, L. J., & Pulciani, M. R. (2019). Minority stress, social support, and the mental health of lesbian, gay, and bisexual Australians during the Australian Marriage law postal survey. *Australian Psychologist, 54*, 336–346.

von Doussa, H., Power, J., & Riggs, D. (2015). Imagining parenthood. *Culture, Health and Sexuality, 17*(9), 1119–1131.

Vygotsky, L. S. (1978). *Mind in society.* Cambridge: Harvard.

Webb, S. N., Kavanagh, P. S., & Chonody, J. M. (2020). Straight, LGB, married, living in sin, children out of wedlock. *Journal of GLBT Family Studies, 16*(1), 66–82.

Worth, P., & Smith, M. (2017). Critical Social Psychology. In N. Brown, T. Lomas, & F. Eiroa-Orosa (Eds.), *The Routledge International Handbook of Critical Positive Psychology.* London: Taylor and Francis.

4 Applying ecological development for LGBTQ+ parents in school contexts

LGBTQ+ parents reflect on: context(s) of uncertainty

I hide any rainbow symbols on me when I enter my daughter's school so she isn't disadvantaged by my sexuality.

(Abigail, 47 yrs, New South Wales)

My child's school is unaware of my orientation and I am not in a relationship.

(Kennedy, 38 yrs, Queensland)

Discrimination is still legal in religious schools so you are never sure how much to disclose.

(Harper, 57 yrs, Victoria)

My experience with the schooling system - and all 3 of my kids are now in high school - is that they are individually supportive of kids who are transitioning or gay and support kids like mine with a parent transitioning but are afraid of saying anything openly. This is not OK... It fosters a sense that there should be shame in being a part of a different family.

(Austin, 53 yrs, Queensland)

4.1 Introduction: policy & context

Research exploring the perspectives of LGBTQ+ parented families in school contexts can generally be divided into three broad categories, empirical research that explores the experiences of LGBTQ+ parents navigating their child's school contexts (e.g. Goldberg, 2014; Leland, 2017; Riggs & Willing, 2013), empirical research exploring the perspectives of the school staff (e.g. teachers and school counsellors) on their opinions and professional practices toward LGBTQ+ parented families (Cloughessy & Waniganayake, 2014; Robinson,

DOI: 10.4324/9781003167471-4

2002), and LGBTQ+ guide research that describes a variety of inclusive strategies that can be adopted by schools to create more welcoming school environments (Fox, 2007; Ryan & Martin, 2000). All three bodies of research tend to be unanimous in arguing that schools often lack policies, procedures and practices inclusive of LGBTQ+ forms of the family (Cloughessy et al., 2019; Ferfolja, 2007; Goldberg, 2014; Robinson, 2002; Ryan & Martin, 2000). Such environments have been associated with a range of negative outcomes for parents including feelings of isolation, marginalisation and exclusion from school contexts, concerns about the potential isolation of their children, and may be a covert form of discrimination that position LGBTQ+ forms of family diversity as 'other', abnormal, deviant and taboo (Robinson & Ferfolja, 2001). However, little empirical research has explored the rate of provision of LGBTQ+ related school supports in school contexts, or the perspective of parents on the perceived importance and benefit of such supports. This chapter discusses the theory of ecological development as a potential lens to deconstruct school contexts, its use in the development of the methodology for this study, and the findings of results regarding aspects of the Individual (participant demographics) and characteristics of school Microsystems (the rate of provision of LGBTQ+ related school supports).

4.2   The theory of ecological development in school contexts

The Theory of Ecological Development (Bronfenbrenner & Crouter, 1983) is a comprehensive framework that can consolidate a range of different aspects of LGBTQ+ parents explored in previous research (see Chapter 3). However, given the wide-ranging environmental contexts that can potentially influence an individual's development, it is not possible to explore the entirety of an ecological system within one study. As such, the study this book reports on explored characteristics of the Individual (LGBTQ+ parents) and LGBTQ+ inclusive aspects of school Microsystems.

Microsystems are contexts or settings which individuals frequently and repetitively engage with. Schools are social institutions parents are mandated to interact with frequently and repeatedly in maintaining the enrolment of their children including activities such as school enrolment, parent-teacher interviews, school community events (sports, concerts), etc. Within a Bronfenbrenner lens, Microsystems are also structured environments that consist of physical, social, and material characteristics that may influence the development of individuals

(Bronfenbrenner & Crouter, 1983). In school contexts, these characteristics include:

- activities,
- interpersonal relationships,
- physical attributes of the schools (location, school type, school level),
- materials and resources accessible within school contexts, and
- school policy/procedures (Bronfenbrenner & Crouter, 1983).

Research exploring parent navigations in school systems has noted various features of these school characteristics related to positive or negative experiences within school environments. These include:

- learning activities and school curriculums that include and represent, or exclude and marginalise, LGBTQ+ parented families;
- interpersonal relationships where school staff are knowledgeable and competent, or have gaps in knowledge and inappropriate stereotypical assumptions, about LGBTQ+ forms of family diversity;
- physical characteristics including metropolitan areas with diverse local communities compared to rural areas and less diverse school communities;
- materials and resources that reflect and represent, or exclude and marginalise, LGBTQ+ parented families; and
- school policies and procedures that explicitly mention and acknowledge LGBTQ+ forms of family diversity, or policies and procedures that assume school community members are heterosexual and fail to accommodate LGBTQ+ parents (Goldberg & Smith, 2014a, 2014b; Kosciw & Diaz, 2008; Lindsay et al., 2006; Ray & Gregory, 2001).

In response to these identified stressful or protective features of schools, school guide literature and LGBTQ+ parent-school research typically recommend schools to include LGBTQ+ inclusive curriculums (such as learning activities and books), staff training in LGBTQ+ parented forms of family diversity, and LGBTQ+ inclusive school policies and procedures (e.g., non-gendered language in school newsletters and enrolment forms; Casper et al., 1992). Yet as Chapter 1 argued, little research has explored the views of LGBTQ+ parents of whether these supports are deemed important and beneficial in creating welcoming school contexts.

This evident gap in the research thus overlooks important informants crucial to the development of LGBTQ+ parent inclusive school policy. Namely, *LGBTQ+ parents themselves*. Thus, the study aimed to explore the views and perspectives of LGBTQ+ parented families in how they would like to be *systematically* represented and accommodated within their child(ren)'s school environment. This focus is justified by the lack of research exploring the perspective of Australian LGBTQ+ parents in developing inclusive evidence-based policy in education, despite inclusive school policy arguing the need to do so (AITSL, 2011). This study attempted to meet the demands for inclusive policy to accommodate the growing LGBTQ+ parents' minority group by supplying statistical and narrative research with the intention of informing policy development and inclusive school practices for the first time in an Australian study. It also sought to embrace the mostly overlooked potential of a positive psychological lens through a Theory of Ecological Development Framework. Therefore, the study endeavoured to meet these gaps in research by answering the following research questions (RQs):

- RQ1: What are Individual characteristics (demographic descriptive statistics) of Australian LGBTQ+ parents and their school Microsystems (in terms of physical and LGBTQ+ supportive features)?
- RQ2: What school supports do Australian LGBTQ+ parents' value or desire in their child(ren)'s schools to create welcoming school environments?
- RQ3: What positive experiences do Australian LGBTQ+ parents derive from their child(ren)'s school communities and what are their suggestions for more inclusive schools?

4.3 Methodology & methods

The study utilised a mixed-method approach adopting qualitative and quantitative measurements in a non-experimental cross-sectional web-based survey, based on an emancipatory methodology in which the research team wished to foreground LGBTQ+ parents' views on their own experiences and needs – rather than institutional views for example. A mix of qualitative and quantitative data has the potential to provide stronger results by drawing on the strengths of each (Creswell & Garrett, 2008) and is endorsed within positive psychological lenses (Vaughan & Rodriguez, 2014). Quantitative techniques were used to measure various characteristics of individuals and school Microsystems, complemented by qualitative techniques to explore the perceived benefits and positive experiences LGBTQ+ parents derive from different characteristics within school Microsystems. Thus, the inclusion of a mixed-method approach enabled a holistic view of Bronfenbrenner's Ecological Theory of Development.

4.3.1 Participants

Participants included 73 LGBTQ+ parents with children currently enrolled in Australian schools. Participants were recruited via social media using paid and unpaid advertising techniques on Facebook.

4.3.2 Measures

4.3.2.1 Survey design

The study consisted of a self-report study recording demographic information of LGBTQ+ parents (Individuals) and the characteristics of school Microsystems. The demographic questionnaire included items measuring different aspects of individuals including age, gender identity, sexual orientation, relationship status, income, residing state, education level, religious denomination, number of children and age of the youngest child. Characteristics of child(ren)'s school Microsystems were gathered using items measuring the type of school, regionality of the school and child(ren)'s grade.

4.3.2.2 Quantitative measurements of supportive school structures

Three quantitative items in the survey measured the provision of supportive strategies within school Microsystems, parents' opinions on the importance perceived of supportive strategies and the perceived benefit of supports in creating welcoming school Microsystems.

Examples of these items included: 'Please indicate to your knowledge if your child's school includes the following supports'. Respondents were requested to respond to each item on a three-point scale (1 = Yes, 2 = No, 3 = Unsure); "Do you think the following supports are important for creating a welcoming environment in your child's school?' (1 = Yes, 2 = No); and 'Do you rate the following supports as beneficial or unproductive in creating a welcoming environment in your child's school?', (1 = Beneficial, 2 = Unproductive). Supportive structures rated included items that reflect LGBTQ+ families in classrooms, mention of LGBTQ+ families in brochures and documents, teacher training in LGBTQ+ topics/issues, LGBTQ+ inclusive forms and specific mention of LGBTQ+ families in school policy.

4.3.2.3 Qualitative measurements of supportive school structures

Five open-ended questions explored participants' perceptions of the benefits of suggested school supports and justification for their inclusion in creating welcoming school Microsystems. Examples of these five items include, 'Do you think teachers being educated about LGBTQ+ family structures and common challenges would benefit your relationship with your child's school? Why or why not?' and 'Do you think lessons and books covering LGBTQ+ information would be beneficial to your experience of your child's school? Why or why not?'. Additional open-ended questions included other school supportive strategies including items that reflect LGBTQ+ families in classrooms, mention of LGBTQ+ families in school brochures and documents as well as school forms that are inclusive of LGBTQ+ parent family structures.

These items were included in the study as previous research on LGBTQ+ parent-school supports adopted predominantly quantitative methods that may overlook the perspectives of the participants under investigation (Bishop & Atlas, 2015; Kosciw & Diaz, 2008). Additionally, qualitative research may prove influential in informing policy development and public opinion by providing descriptive narratives of perceptions and experiences with social organisations (Lambert, 2005; Vaughan & Rodrigues, 2014).

4.3.2.4 Positive experiences in schools

Positive experiences were pro-actively explored in application of the positive psychology lens outlined in Chapter Three, and to ensure the deficit model so common to LGBTQ+ studies was not applied. This exploration of positive experiences was facilitated via two open-ended questions that requested participants to indicate whether they had positive and inclusive experiences with their child's school and to give examples. These items are further built on strength-based psychological research to explore possible supports that may diminish identified challenges LGBTQ+ parents experience in school environments. Examples of these items include, 'Have you had any positive experiences with your child's school or teacher as an LGBTQ+ parent? Please explain/give examples' and 'Has your child's school included your family in some way as an LGBTQ+ parented family? Please explain/give examples'.

4.3.2.5 Suggestions for Schools

Finally, participants were asked to respond to an open-ended question 'Please list any suggestions you have for schools or teachers, in terms of making LGBTQ+ parented families feel more welcome in your child's school community'. This item was included to explore and gain insight into the opinions of LGBTQ+ parents on desired characteristics within their child(ren)'s school contexts (Goldberg, 2014).

4.3.3 Procedures

The Qualtrics survey included participant information and consent forms notifying participants of confidentiality, implied consent, selection criteria and a brief background to the study. The 20-minute online Qualtrics survey was anonymous and voluntary consisting of 18 closed-ended items as well as eight open-ended items.

4.4 Data analysis

4.4.1 Quantitative analysis (descriptive)

The quantitative analysis component of this study comprised creating frequency tables and graphs for 18 closed-ended items included in the survey through the Qualtrics data analysis. Descriptive data were then tabulated in figures relating to Bronfenbrenner's ecological levels including characteristics of the Individual. Namely, LGBTQ+ parents and their child(ren), physical characteristics of school Microsystems, LGBTQ+ support structures provided within school Microsystems, as well as LGBTQ+ parent opinions on the importance and benefit of supportive strategies within school Microsystems.

4.4.2 Qualitative analysis (thematic and Leximancer-driven)

The qualitative analysis included two approaches. These were researcher-driven qualitative thematic analysis applying Bronfenbrenner's concepts, and utilisation of Leximancer computer software.

4.5 Ethical considerations

Ethics approval was granted by the Human Research Ethics Committee (HREC) at Macquarie University. An important ethical consideration made for the study was to support the anonymity of participants and the confidentiality of the people in their contexts – no identifying information was requested, and any identifying information offered was removed. Pseudonyms have been used in all direct reporting of quotes.

4.6 LGBTQ+ parents' characteristics and school Microsystems characteristics

The first research question informing the study considered characteristics of Individuals and their Microsystems. This section of the chapter outlines detailed descriptive statistics of participants, physical characteristics of their schools, and supportive structures in school environments.

4.6.1 Individual-level characteristics – LGBTQ+ parent demographic diversity

The demographic characteristics of LGBTQ+ parent survey participants are shown in Table 4.1. The age of participants ranged from 25 to 64 years. Almost half of the samples were 35–44 years. Participants were mostly located in eastern states; primarily Queensland followed by N.S.W, Victoria, S.A, W.A and the N.T. The gender of parents in the sample was predominantly female followed by male, other and transgender. Of those who responded 'other', four respondents identified as non-binary, one as trans-male, one as trans-female and one as female-bodied. Most participants identified as lesbian followed by 'another option', gay and bisexual. Of participants who responded 'another option', four identified as queer, three as pansexual, two as trans and one as bisexual polyamorous.

The sample was predominantly affluent and highly educated. Nearly 70% of the sample earned annual incomes over $90,000 and over 60% held university (undergraduate and postgraduate) qualifications. Close to 70% of the participants were in married or committed relationships followed by divorced, another option and single. Of those participants selecting 'another option', five were dating, three were single and one was in a polyamorous relationship.

Table 4.1 shows over half of the participants identified their religious/spiritual belief as Atheist, followed by Christianity, another option, Agnostic/undecided, Judaism, and Islam. Of the four indicating another option, six identified as pagan, two as none, one as yoga and one as ex-Christian. Most participants indicated having two or more children. The age of participants' youngest child ranged from 0 to 18 years; most children were aged under 14 years.

Table 4.1 Frequency Distribution of Participant Demographic Characteristics (*n* = 73)

Characteristic	%		%
Age		*Income*	
25–34 years	16.4	<$30,000	8.2
35–44 years	48.0	$30,000–59,999	8.2
45–54 years	31.5	$60,000–89,999	13.7
55–64 years	4.1	Over $90,000	67.1
Gender		Prefer not to say	2.7
Female	72.6	*Education*	
Male	12.3	Up to four years high school	2.4
Transgender	5.5	Completed high school	9.6
Another option	9.6	Diploma or certificate	21.9
Sexual Orientation		Undergraduate university degree	24.7
Lesbian	61.6	Postgraduate university degree	41.1
Another option	13.7	*Religion*	
Gay	12.3	Christianity	14.5
Bisexual	12.3	Judaism	1.5
Relationship Status		Islam	1.5
Single, never married	4.1	Atheist/None	56.5
Married, committed de		Agnostic/Undecided	11.6
facto relationship	68.5	Another option	14.5
Divorced, separated	15.1	*Age of Youngest Child*	
Another option	12.3	0–4 years	27.4
State		5–9 years	42.5
New South Wales	23.3	10–14 years	23.3
Northern Territory	1.4	15–18 years	6.8
Queensland	37.0	*Number of Children*	
South Australia	9.6	1	31.5
Victoria	23.3	2	39.7
Western Australia	5.5	3 or more	28.8

4.6.2 School Microsystem characteristics

The characteristics of school environments or Microsystems were explored in two ways. First, in relation to their physical characteristics and second, the provision of LGBTQ+ related supportive structures in schools (such as inclusive curriculum, teacher training and non-gendered enrolment forms).

4.6.2.1 Physical Microsystem characteristics

Teachers have been noted to make assumptions that LGBTQ+ parents may not be present within school contexts, and as such are not required to be included or accommodated within school practices (Kozik-Rosabal, 2000; Robinson, 2002). As LGBTQ+ parents may not disclose their sexual orientation or gender identity in school contexts (Casper et al., 1992), it was important to explore what types of school levels, locations and types LGBTQ+ parents have their children enrolled. In terms of physical characteristics, LGBTQ+ parents have children enrolled in all forms of schooling, grade levels and location types as highlighted in Table 4.2. Although most participants had children enrolled in public schools, metropolitan areas and primary or elementary school levels.

4.6.2.2 LGBTQ+ related school supports

The supportive school characteristics provided to participants were explored by asking LGBTQ+ parents' awareness of their child's school providing supportive strategies identified in school guide research. Namely, LGBTQ+ inclusive (non-gendered) school forms, items that

Table 4.2 Frequency Distribution of Child's School Characteristics ($n = 73$)

Category	%
Child's School Type	
Public	69.9
Independent	13.7
Catholic	13.7
Other	2.7
Child's Grade	
Kindergarten/Preparatory	17.8
1–3	30.1
4–6	36.9
7–10	8.2
11–12	6.9
Location of School	
Inner Metropolitan	28.8
Outer Metropolitan	35.6
Regional	31.5
Rural/Remote	4.1

reflect LGBTQ+ families (e.g., posters and rainbow flags), specific mention of LGBTQ+ families in school policy, teacher training in LG-BTQ+ topics/issues, and lessons on LGBTQ+ topics or issues. As can be seen in Figure 4.1, the provision of LGBTQ+ related school supports in Australia was relatively low. Inclusive school forms were the most common supportive strategy present in schools followed by items that reflect LGBTQ+ families in classrooms, specific mention of LG-BTQ+ families in school policy, teacher training in LGBTQ+ parented families, lessons on LGBTQ+ topics and mention of LGBTQ+ family structures in school brochures/documents. Parents were more likely to indicate school environments did not include such supports and there was a high level of uncertainty in whether school contexts offered these supports, particularly regarding teacher training in LGBTQ+ forms of family structures.

4.7 Discussion

Schools, teachers, and other school staff have been noted to hold various negative assumptions, inaccurate beliefs, and lack of knowledge of LGBTQ+ parented families (Robinson, 2002). Previous research has also noted that schools and teachers can tend to adopt reactive measures in responding to LGBTQ+ parented families where parents are required to 'come-out' in schools to receive LGBTQ+ inclusive practices and procedures (Byard et al., 2013; Casper et al., 1992). As not all LGBTQ+ parents disclose their sexual orientations or gender identities within school contexts (Casper et al., 1992; Goldberg, 2014), the

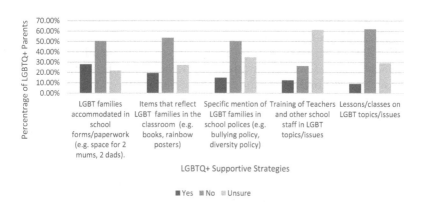

Figure 4.1 Support strategies reported by Australian LGBTQ+ parents in schools (n = 73).

study sought to explore different aspects of parents and family structures in an effort to advocate this information to school community members and policy developers without the requirement for parents to disclose their family structures within school contexts.

This chapter highlighted various aspects of school Microsystems found to be important in creating welcoming school contexts from previous LGBTQ+ parent-school research, explored the Individual characteristics of LGBTQ+ parent families and the provision of LGBTQ+ related school supports in Australian schools. The study found that the sample of LGBTQ+ parents were mainly lesbian Caucasian mothers consisting of higher incomes and educational levels reflective of previous LGBTQ+ family research (Crouch et al., 2014; Power et al., 2010). Parents had children enrolled in all school types, school locations and schooling levels. Parents also noted relatively low rates of provision of LGBTQ+ related supports in school contexts.

Although LGBTQ+ parents' ratings of school supportive features has been questioned as potentially ill-informed of actual service provision (Bishop & Atlas, 2015), from the perspective of parents, Australian school environments do not commonly include advocated LGBTQ+ related inclusive practices, consistent with international research (Bishop & Atlas, 2015; Kosciw & Diaz, 2008). Yet any Australian teacher could be made to teach on sexuality and gender, both directly and indirectly, and their comfort with LGBTQ+ themes was low (Ezer et al., 2021). Also, similarly to previous international research, the study found that school forms were the most common method of support provided by schools (Bishop & Atlas, 2015). It found parents were largely unaware of whether teachers were trained specifically in LGBTQ+ forms of family diversity (Kosciw & Diaz, 2008; McDonald & Morgan, 2019). Also consistent with previous research (Robinson, 2002), Australian educational policy rarely included explicit mention of LGBTQ+ parented families and tended to privilege other forms of diversity such as multiculturalism, ethnicities, English as another language and disabilities (see the first chapter of this book).

The findings offer empirical evidence supportive of previous research arguing that school contexts commonly lack inclusive school practices, procedures and policies that accommodate or reflect LGBTQ+ parented families (Ferfolja, 2007; Lindsay et al., 2006; Robinson, 2002). Research exploring LGBTQ+ parent experiences in schools has consistently reported school environments that lack inclusive school practices and procedures that accommodate or reflect LGBTQ+ parented families as challenging Microsystem characteristics for LGBTQ+ parents (Casper et al., 1992; Goldberg, 2014; Goldberg &

Smith, 2014a; Kosciw & Diaz, 2008). Rather than overtly discriminating or stigmatising LGBTQ+ parents, such school contexts have been argued to exclude and inadvertently 'other' LGBTQ+ parented families (Casper et al., 1992). As a result, school community members may not be offered educational opportunities to address possible misconceptions or commonly held stereotypical beliefs and inadvertently encourage a lack of awareness of LGBTQ+ forms of family diversity (Casper et al., 1992; Goldberg & Smith, 2014b). Such 'gaps' in the knowledge of school communities have been attributed to experiences of 'clumsiness' in school staff when dealing with LGBTQ+ parents (Goldberg et al., 2017), points of exclusion for students of LGBTQ+ parents (Ray & Gregory, 2001) and encourages feelings of marginalisation or invisibility in parents (Kosciw & Diaz, 2008).

The low rate of provision of LGBTQ+ related supports has previously been related to various physical characteristics of schools including geographical location (Metropolitan vs. Rural; Lindsay et al., 2006), local community socio-demographic contexts (Casper et al., 1992), individual school community members stance on LGBTQ+ identities (Robinson, 2002) and representation of other LGBTQ+ parented families in schools (Goldberg, 2014). Other potential explanations for the lack of provision of school supports include highly charged debates within religious and political arenas regarding the inclusion of such supports in schools (Law, 2017; UNESCO, 2016), and the lack of educational policies that accommodate and explicitly include LGBTQ+ identities within school contexts (Robinson & Ferfolja, 2001). The dearth of strategic explicit instructions on inclusive practices may prove particularly problematic in the highly politicised and intensely debated rights of LGBTQ+ identities within schools (e.g. Safe Schools, same-sex marriage postal vote) as schools may be concerned about the realistic potential for schools to receive political and social backlash to progressively inclusive practices, thus deeming such supports as too 'controversial' (Ferfolja & Ullman, 2017). Speaking to school-based key informants could be the next step in understanding the provisions beyond parents' perceptions, though answers might be highly politicised in the current environment. However, given that Australian LGBTQ+ parents are now recognised legally and accepted widely by general society (Australian Bureau of Statistics/ABS, 2016), there is an evident need to build more inclusive and explicit school policy regarding LGBTQ+ parented families.

In contrast to previous international studies (Kosciw & Diaz, 2008), this study indicates LGBTQ+ parents may prefer public educational systems over private or independent schools, and is consistent with

Australian national samples (ABS, 2018). Research exploring the experiences of LGBTQ+ parents within school contexts have highlighted parents as being purposive in school selection favouring diversity in schools and inclusive supportive features (Bower, 2008; Casper et al., 1992; Goldberg & Smith, 2014a). In contrast to international settings (Kosciw & Diaz, 2008; Leland, 2017), Australian public schools may be viewed as a more inclusive and diverse educational alternative compared to private or independent systems. Although, future research is required to explore Australian LGBTQ+ parents' experiences and considerations in selecting schools for their children.

4.8 Summary of key points

The main ideas that can be drawn from this work include:

• LGBTQ+ parents are present within all school types, school levels and school locations,
• Australian Educational Policy does not typically explicitly include LGBTQ+ forms of family diversity,
• School contexts generally fail to include commonly advocated LGBTQ+ related school supports,
• School contexts that lack supportive structures have been related to negative outcomes in LGBTQ+ families.
• Negative outcomes for LGBTQ+ families include potential 'othering' or marginalisation of parents and potential points of exclusion for their children.

4.9 Conclusion & next chapter

This chapter discussed how Australian LGBTQ+ parents were largely highly educated with high incomes typical of previous research; accessed all types of school levels and areas; and found these often failed to include LGBTQ+ inclusive policies, procedures, and practices. The next chapter discusses more specifically parents' views and justifications for the importance of LGBTQ+ related features in their children's schooling Microsystems.

References

ABS. (2016, June 11). *6224.055 Labour force, Australia.* Retrieved from: www.abs.gov.au
ABS. (2018, March 8). *4221.0 Schools, Australia 2018.* Retrieved from: ww.abs.gov.au

Australian Institute for Teaching and School Leadership. (2011). *Australian Professional Standards for Teaching.* Retrieved from https://www.aitsl.edu.au/teach/standards

Bishop, C. M., & Atlas, J. G. (2015). School curriculum, policies, and practices regarding lesbian, gay, bisexual, and transgender families. *Education and Urban Society, 47*(7), 766–784.

Bower, L. (2008). Standing up for diversity. *Kappa Delta Pi Record, 44*(4), 181–183.

Bronfenbrenner, U., & Crouter, A. (1983). The evolution of environmental models in developmental research. In P. Mussen & W. Kessen (Eds.), *Handbook of Child Psychology Volume 1* (pp. 357–414). New York: John Wiley.

Byard, E., Kosciw, J., & Bartkiewicz, M. (2013). *Schools and LGBT-parent families.* In A. E. Goldberg & K. R. Allen (Eds.), *LGBT-parent families* (pp. 275–290). New York: Springer.

Casper, V., Schultz, S., & Wickens, E. (1992). Breaking the silences. *Teachers College Record, 94*(1), 109–137.

Cloughessy, K., & Waniganayake, M. (2014). Early childhood educators working with children who have lesbian, gay, bisexual and transgender parents: What does the literature tell us? *Early Child Development and Care, 184*(8), 1267–1280.

Cloughessy, K., Waniganayake, M., & Blatterer, H. (2019). The good and the bad. *Journal of Research in Childhood Education, 33*(3), 446–458.

Creswell, J., & Garrett, A. L. (2008). The "movement" of mixed methods research and the role of educators. *South African Journal of Education, 28*(3), 321–333.

Cresswell, J., & Plano Clark, V. (2011). Choosing a mixed methods design. In J. Cresswell & V. Plano Clark (Eds.), *Designing and Conducting Mixed Method Research* (pp. 53–106). Los Angeles: SAGE.

Crouch, S. R., Waters, E., McNair, R., Power, J., & Davis, E. (2014). Parent-reported measures of child health and wellbeing in same-sex parent families. *BMC Public Health, 14*(1), 635–635.

Ezer, P., Fisher, C. M., Jones, T. & Power, J. (2021). Changes in sexuality education teacher training since the release of the Australian curriculum. *Sexuality Research and Social Policy, 12*(3), 119–143.

Ferfolja, T. (2007). Schooling cultures. *International Journal of Inclusive Education, 11*(2), 147–162.

Ferfolja, T., & Ullman, J. (2017). Gender and sexuality in education and health. *Sex Education, 17*(3), 235–241.

Fox, R. K. (2007). One of the hidden diversities in schools. *Childhood Education, 83*(5), 277–281.

Goldberg, A. E. (2014). Lesbian, gay, and heterosexual adoptive parents' experiences in preschool environments. *Early Childhood Research Quarterly, 29*(4), 669–681.

Goldberg, A. E., & Smith, J. Z. (2014a). Perceptions of stigma and self-reported school engagement in same-sex couples with young children. *Psychology of Sexual Orientation and Gender Diversity, 1*(3), 202–212.

Goldberg, A. E., & Smith, J. Z. (2014b). Preschool selection considerations and experiences of school mistreatment among lesbian, gay, and heterosexual adoptive parents. *Early Childhood Research Quarterly, 29*(1), 64–75.

Goldberg, A., Black, K., Sweeney, K., & Moyer, A. (2017). Lesbian, gay and heterosexual adoptive parents' perceptions of inclusivity and receptiveness in early childhood education settings. *Journal of Research in Childhood Education, 31*(1), 141–159.

Kosciw, J. G., & Diaz, E. M. (2008). *Involved, Invisible, Ignored.* New York: GLSEN.

Kozik-Rosabal, G. (2000). "Well, we haven'tnoticed anything bad going on," Said the principal. *Education and Urban Society, 32*(3), 368–389.

Law, B. (2017). Moral panic 101. *Quarterly Essay, 67*, 1–80.

Leland, A. S. (2017). Navigating gay fatherhood. *Gender and Education, 29*(5), 632–647.

Lindsay, J., Perlesz, A., Brown, R., McNair, R., De Vaus, D., & Pitts, M. (2006). Stigma or respect. *Sociology, 40*(6), 1059–1077.

McDonald, I., & Morgan, G. (2019). Same-sex parents' experiences of schools in England. *Journal of GLBT Family Studies, 15*(5), 486–500.

Power, J., Perlesz, A., Brown, R., Schofield, M., Pitts, M., McNair, R., & Bickerdike, A. (2010). Diversity, tradition and family. *Gay and Lesbian Issues and Psychology Review, 6*(2), 66.

Ray, V., & Gregory, R. (2001). School experiences of the lesbian and gay. *Family Matters, 59*, 28–34.

Riggs, D. W., & Willing, I. (2013). They're all just little bits, aren't they. *Journal of Australian Studies, 37*(3), 364–377.

Robinson, K. (2002). Making the invisible visible. *Contemporary Issues in Early Childhood, 3*(3), 415–434.

Robinson, K., & Ferfolja, T. (2001). What are we doing this for? *British Journal of Sociology of Education, 22*(1), 121–133.

Ryan, D., & Martin, A. (2000). Lesbian, gay, bisexual, and transgender parents in the school systems. *School Psychology Review, 29*(2), 207–216.

UNESCO. (2016). *Out In The Open: Education Sector Responses to Violence based on Sexual Orientation and Gender Identity/Expression.* Paris: UNESCO.

Vaughan, M. D., & Rodriguez, E. M. (2014). LGBT strengths. *Psychology of Sexual Orientation and Gender Diversity, 1*(4), 325–334.

5 Foregrounding LGBTQ+ parents' perspectives on school supports

LGBTQ+ parents reflect on: relationships of policies to supports
Department needs to review the controversial issues policy and remove gay as a controversial issue.

(Lucas, 37 yrs, New South Wales)

Make it mandatory that administrations have professional development in this area and that all schools create a policy.

(Danielle, 36 yrs, Queensland)

A diversity and inclusion statement on the website and school brochure that specifically mentions Lgbti families would be a great sign.

(Harper, 57 yrs, Victoria)

Show a diversity policy in parent handbook material that speaks about LGBTQI children and families. Have a day where they talk about LGBT issues to kids, but in a fun way, books, drag queen storytime. Also celebrate pride days or IDAHOBIT etc.

(Rylee, 34 yrs, Queensland)

5.1 Introduction: LGBTQ+ inclusive school supports

The previous chapter highlighted that Australian school *Microsystems* or contexts do not commonly include LGBTQ+ related school supports. These findings are similar to previous global research which has noted that school environments tend to lack school policies, procedures and practices that reflect or include LGBTQ+ forms of diversity (UNESCO, 2016). As a result, schools have been largely argued as settings that inadvertently marginalise and exclude LGBTQ+ forms of family diversity and render them as invisible forms of diversity (Robinson, 2002; UNESCO, 2016). In recognition of these challenges, various guides (Bower & Klecka, 2009; Ryan & Martin, 2000; UNESCO, 2016)

DOI: 10.4324/9781003167471-5

and researchers (Cloughessy et al., 2019; Goldberg, 2014; Goldberg et al., 2017; Leland, 2017) have suggested similar strategies to overcome the potential marginalisation of LGBTQ+ parents in schools. The recommendations to improve school Microsystems or contexts are similar in arguing for schools to include teacher training in LGBTQ+ related topics and issues, learning activities and classroom materials that reflect LGBTQ+ parented families, enrolment forms that accommodate LGBTQ+ parent family formations and the explicit inclusion of LGBTQ+ parents in school policies and documents (Casper et al., 1992).

Yet, these supports are often advocated for in response to the identified challenges parents experience in school contexts and have not included the perspective of parents on 'if and why' such supports are important in creating welcoming school environments. Researchers (Herbstrith & Busse, 2020; Leland, 2017), and education policy concerning diversity (Australian Institute for Teaching and School Leadership/AITSL, 2011), similarly suggest that schools and teachers should reach out to representatives of minority groups to inform the development of inclusive school policies and practices. Generally, this is seen as a method to ensure policy is developed in a respectful and culturally sensitive way for the minority group they are intended to serve. However, such consultative approaches may prove difficult for teachers and educational professionals as not all LGBTQ+ parents disclose their identity within school Microsystems (Lindsay et al., 2006).

To overcome this challenge, this book, based on an Australian study, has sought to explore LGBTQ+ parents views on how they would like to be included and represented within school contexts using an online anonymous survey. The following section highlights the use of the Theory of Ecological Development as a framework to explore LGBTQ+ related supports in school environments (Section 5.1), parents' perceptions of the importance and benefit of these supports in creating more welcoming school contexts (Section 5.2) and a discussion of the findings related to previous research (Section 5.3).

5.2 LGBTQ+ related school supports as characteristics of school Microsystems

The Theory of Ecological Developments states the environment is influential in the development of an individual and can be deconstructed into five overarching layers. The Microsystem includes institutional and social contexts individuals repeatedly interact with during their lifespan. The Mesosystem includes the influence of at least two settings in the development of the Individual, such as work and school contexts. The Exosystem conceptualises distal factors that may influence an individual's development which an individual is unable to control and are less frequently exposed to forums such as mass media. The Macrosystem encapsulates broad social attitudes and ideologies of the culture in which individuals develop and the chronosystem denotes how these systems continually change over time.

The third and fourth chapters of the book showed how conceptualisation of Microsystems offers a potentially useful framework to deconstruct school environments into key LGBTQ+ related inclusive characteristics commonly advocated by LGBTQ+ parent-school research, and explored the perspectives of parents on the perceived need for such supports (Bronfenbrenner & Crouter, 1983). Microsystems (or schools) are structured environments that consist of physical, social and material characteristics that can influence the development of an individual (Bronfenbrenner & Crouter, 1983). These characteristics can include activities, interpersonal relationships, materials, and resources accessible within school contexts and school procedures. When viewed alongside the recommendations and suggestions recommended by previous LGBTQ+ parents within school research (e.g. Casper et al., 1992), various characteristics of school Microsystems are advocated to create more welcoming and inclusive school environments for LGBTQ+ forms of family diversity. These include:

- Interpersonal Relationships – Educational staff competent in LGBTQ+ parent topics and issues,
- School Procedures – School enrolment forms inclusive of LGBTQ+ family constellations,
- Materials and Resources – Posters and flags that represent LGBTQ+ parent forms of family diversity,
- School Policies – Explicit mention of LGBTQ+ parents in school documents and websites,
- Activities – Lesson and Curriculums that include and represent LGBTQ+ parented families.

5.3 LGBTQ+ parents' perceptions supportive features in school Microsystems

The second research question of this study considered LGBTQ+ parents' perceptions of the benefit and importance of supportive strategies in creating welcoming school environments. This was explored via two quantitative measures of perceived importance and benefit of supportive structures in schools and open-ended qualitative justifications for why supportive structures may, or may not, be important in creating welcoming school environments. The following section describes results from the quantitative measures on LGBTQ+ parents' perceptions on supportive strategies within schools (Section 5.2.1), Leximancer analysis of responses to the importance of staff training on LGBTQ+ parented families (Section 5.2.2), LGBTQ+ inclusive forms (Section 5.2.3), items and materials that reflect LGBTQ+ parented families (Section 5.2.4), explicit mention of LGBTQ+ families in school websites and brochures (Section 5.2.5), and LGBTQ+ inclusive curricula (Section 5.2.6).

5.3.1 Perceived importance and benefit of supportive structures in school Microsystems

The second research question of this study considered LGBTQ+ parents' perceptions of the value of supportive strategies in creating welcoming school environments. This was explored via two quantitative measures of the perceived importance and benefit of supportive structures in schools. As shown in Table 5.1, over 80% of participants deemed all supportive strategies as important and beneficial in forming positive school environments. Participants were unanimous in deeming school staff training in LGBTQ+ topics and LGBTQ+ inclusive forms as particularly pertinent in creating welcoming school environments, followed by items reflecting LGBTQ+ families in classrooms, mention of LGBTQ+ families in brochures/documents, explicit mention in school policy and lessons/classes on LGBTQ+ topics/issues. Results indicate that all supportive strategies are perceived to be of some value in creating welcoming school Microsystems.

While the study does indicate that LGBTQ+ parents value all supports, the quantitative nature of the measurements offers a limited view into the perspective of parents in their opinions and justifications for each support. As such, parents responded to open-ended questions that asked participants to justify why each support was a valued characteristic in school contexts. The following section highlights the thematic analysis of parents' views of why, or why not, such supports are deemed valuable characteristics in school Microsystems. Using the directives of Braun and Clarke (2006), the two most dominant, and least dominant themes identified by Leximancer are highlighted and discusses.

Table 5.1 Perceived Importance and Benefit of Supportive Structures in
School Environments (*n* = 73)

Support Strategies	LGBTQ+ Parent Perceptions of School Supportive Strategies			
	Importance		Benefit	
	Yes	No	Beneficial	Unproductive
Teacher training	100.0%	*	100.0%	*
LGBTQ+ inclusive forms	100.0%	*	100.0%	*
Items that reflect LGBTQ+ Families	95.9%	4.1%	95.9%	4.1%
LGBTQ+ families in website	86.3%	13.7%	90.4%	9.6%
LGBTQ+ inclusive school Policies	83.6%	16.4%	90.4%	9.6%
LGBTQ+ inclusive curriculum	80.8%	19.2%	88.7%	11.3%

5.3.2 *Leximancer analysis of justifications for teacher training in LGBTQ+ parented family structures in school environments*

In the survey, participants were asked 'Do you think teachers being educated about LGBTQ+ family structures and common challenges would benefit your relationship with your child's school? Why or why not?'. The Leximancer map (Figure 5.1) and content analysis report indicate the dominant themes were 'family' (56 Hits), 'school (28 Hits), 'feel' (24 Hits), 'inclusive' (10 Hits) and 'unsure' (6 Hits).

5.3.2.1 *'Family' staff training justifications*

The first theme Leximancer identified, 'family', was composed of arguments that school staff training in LGBTQ+ families; should be included within the education of all forms of family diversity, may normalise LGBTQ+ parented families as a recognised form of family diversity and may aid in supporting children of LGBTQ+ parented families. Leximancer selected typical quotes for this theme include:

> ... it should be embedded in being educated in broader not common family structures, ie accepting of diverse family structures not just LGBTQ+
>
> (Clara, 45 yrs, VIC)

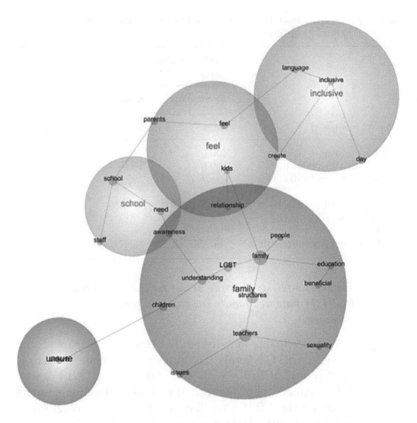

Figure 5.1 Leximancer map of LGBTQ+ parents' justification for teacher training on LGBTQ+ family structures in school contexts (*n* = 69).

…it may assist normalize LGBTQ+ families for teachers however there is a risk that education like this becomes tokenistic. LGBTQ+ families are as diverse as any other family there is a risk that assumptions are made. For example, many people assume that our kids are from a previous relationship and there are multiple parents involved as this is a "common challenge" for LGBTQ+ families. This is not the case for us. Education on inclusivity would be beneficial [in understanding] language and ideas … to manage education on families, that is inclusive events like mother's day and father's day. Avoidance of this stuff is not the answer.

(Elisabeth, 37 yrs, QLD)

I think it's important for teachers to understand the differences and similarities of our family to help other children/families to have an awareness and to facilitate any difficulties my children might encounter.

(Karen, 43 yrs, VIC)

5.3.2.2 'School' staff training justifications

The second most dominant theme identified by Leximancer was 'school'. Justifications within this theme included arguments that LG-BTQ+ competency in school staff may overcome challenging social interactions, raise awareness of family diversity and address identified knowledge gaps in teacher knowledge. Leximancer selected the following quotes as exemplars of this theme:

...approaching the staff regarding LGBTQ+ issues would not need to include a social skills lesson first.

(Cynthia, 26 yrs, QLD)

Sometimes people just need a little awareness. The smallest changes can make families feel included and welcomed. E.g teachers realising that when a child brings home two Mother's day cards, that makes the whole family feel accepted, included and like they're part of the community.

(Cora, 32 yrs, South Australia)

... definitely because being a Catholic school, the awareness of challenges faced by LGBTQ+ parents is very low among staff, and perpetuates over time.

(Stephanie, 42 yrs, South Australia)

5.3.2.3 'Unsure' staff training justifications

The most unique theme identified by Leximancer was 'unsure' which comprised of arguments that teacher training in LGBTQ+ parented families may overcome LGBTQ+ parent uncertainties within school environments. Namely, concerns about the provision of support given to students after coming out and the response of school staff to the disclosure of family constellations. For example, Meghan (35 yrs, QLD) said *'because I try to not be noticed at the school because I'm unsure if there would be any support for my son'*, Evelyn (27 yrs, QLD) said '...
because teachers are often shocked or unsure with how to react when

learning that my children have two mothers'; and Fran (48 yrs, SA) said *'I think we have educated our children's teachers, year by year, simply by our doggedly unsensational presence. Our school is not threatened by us, as we are one family structure of many. However, I am unsure whether all the school staff are as comfortable with us as I hope. Education would expose the cracks'.* The themes identified by Leximancer thus indicated that teacher competence in LGBTQ+ parented families is a desired aspect of LGBTQ+ parent-school Microsystems. Justifications for teacher competency in LGBTQ+ parented families in school contexts include educating school staff about all forms of family diversity, addressing knowledge gaps in teachers and potentially alleviating concerns of disclosure of LGBTQ+ family structures.

5.3.3 Leximancer analysis of justifications for LGBTQ+ inclusive forms in school environments

Participants were also asked 'Do you think forms and documents that allow for different family structures (e.g., two mums and two dads) would be beneficial to your relationship with your child's school? Why or why not?'. The Leximancer map (Figure 5.2) and content analysis report indicate the dominant themes identified by Leximancer were 'forms' (46 Hits), 'families (32 Hits), 'feel' (13 Hits), 'inclusive' (7 Hits), 'accepting' (4 Hits) and 'gender' (4 Hits).

5.3.3.1 'Forms' form inclusion justifications

Leximancer identified the dominant theme within the qualitative data as 'forms'. This theme included evidence of parents having to adapt forms, evidence of schools providing inclusive forms and value in forms reflecting all types of family diversity. Example extracts from Leximancer include:

> I often have to modify forms in order to accurately describe the relationship between my son and my partner. Inclusive forms are also helpful for single parents, step-parents, foster carers and indigenous families.
>
> (Harper, 57 yrs, VIC)

> My school already has that. It just says name and relationship to student. it also caters for other family structures. grandparents/foster carers/other family.
>
> (Beatrice, 39 yrs, QLD)

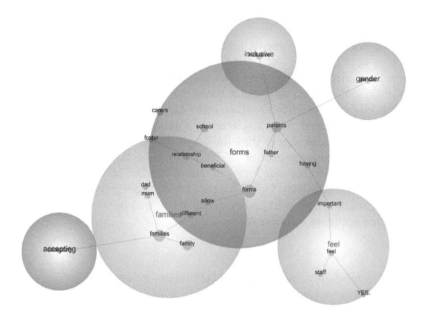

Figure 5.2 Leximancer map of LGBTQ+ parents' justifications for inclusive school forms in school Microsystems (*n* = 69).

Forms can easily be gender inclusive (simple language such as parent) and can help make those filling in the form more comfortable.

(Tom, 49 yrs, QLD)

5.3.3.2 'Families' form inclusion justifications

The second most dominant theme identified by Leximancer was 'families'. This theme included examples of how non-inclusive school forms can pose unique challenges to LGBTQ+ parents. Leximancer extracted quotes typical of this theme include:

It's just basic discrimination to be honest. With the diversity of families why do our forms all have mum and dad on them? It says that LGBTQ+ or any family without a mum or dad are not ok.

(Elisabeth, 37 yrs, QLD)

It is incredibly offensive to assume each family is made up of a mum and dad. We intentionally rewrite forms at our child's school.

(Ivy, 39 yrs, VIC)

5.3.3.3 'Gender' form inclusion justifications

The least dominant theme was named 'gender' by Leximancer. This theme contained arguments highlighting the non-issue when parent forms were LGBTQ+ inclusive and negative experiences when forms were not adequately inclusive. For example, Mia (48 yrs, VIC) stated *'I'm tired of crossing out gender specific titles'*, Aiden (47 yrs, SA) responded *'they generally are non-gender specific anyway'* and Brittany (47 yrs, VIC) stated *'our school is about parents not gender'*. The themes identified by Leximancer thus indicated that inclusive forms were a desired and valued aspect of LGBTQ+ parent-school Microsystems. Justifications for inclusive forms in school contexts include being conditional on inclusivity for all forms of family diversity, overcoming exclusionary experiences and evidence of the 'non-issue' when schools provide adequate inclusive forms.

5.3.4 Parents' perceptions of LGBTQ+ related posters and flags in school contexts

Participants were afforded the option to further elaborate on their views or opinions on the importance of LGBTQ+ posters and flags (displays) by responding to the question 'Do you think the use of LGBTQ+ objects in your child's school such as rainbow flags and posters that reflect LGBTQ+-parented families would improve your experience of your child's school? Why or why not?'. As can be seen in Figure 5.3, five dominant themes were identified in Leximancer, including – 'families' (41 Hits), 'school' (41 Hits), 'diversity' (25 Hits), 'students' (19 Hits) and 'people' (6 Hits). Leximancer content analysis identified various opinions on the benefits of rainbow flags and posters that represent LGBTQ+ families in strengthening parent-school relationships.

5.3.4.1 'Families' display justifications

In this theme, exemplary quotes identified by Leximancer highlighted concerns and support regarding the benefit of LGBTQ+ family-related posters and rainbow flags in creating welcoming school environments. Dominant themes emergent from LGBTQ+ parents' opinions on the benefit of LGBTQ+-related posters in creating welcoming schools included concerns that posters and flags may lack any meaningful change in creating welcoming schools and may be

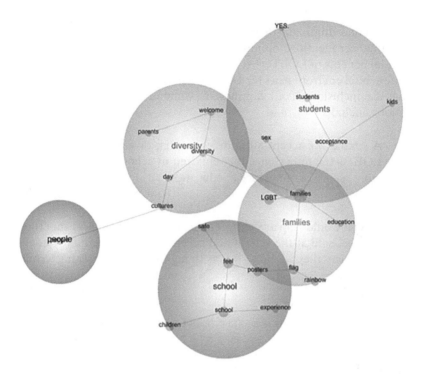

Figure 5.3 Leximancer map of LGBTQ+ parents' justification for the inclusion of posters and flags in school Microsystems (*n* = 73).

symbology or iconography not relevant to some families. Leximancer identified quotes included:

> It's how people are treated that's important. A rainbow flag isn't a good indication of the way the staff at the school respond to LGBTQ+ families.
>
> (Monica, 36 yrs old, WA)

> Our family doesn't really participate in LGBTQ+ activities so I don't feel posters and objects would make a difference in our children's school experience.
>
> (Irene, 48 yrs old, QLD)

> I don't think a flag is necessary but LGBTQ+ posters, books would help my child feel their family is the norm.
>
> (Kelly, 36 yrs old, NSW)

5.3.4.2 'School' display justifications

The second dominant theme identified by Leximancer was 'school'. Leximancer identified opinions within this theme highlighted the potential benefits of LGBTQ+ related posters and rainbow flags to signal safe school environments for LGBTQ+ parented families, provisional on the inclusion of all families. Leximancer identified exemplary quotes included:

> A simple 'we accept all families' poster, or similar, would allow LGBTQ+ families enrolling children at school to feel safer and more secure in our choice of education enrolment.
>
> (Carmen, 27 yrs old, NSW)

> I feel it would help any children including my own know that they can feel safe at the school and accepted if they eventually come out as gay they wouldn't feel as though there is something wrong with them.
>
> (Alex, 28 yrs old, QLD)

> It just feels like this is a safe school to send your child to.
>
> (Ivy, 39 yrs old, VIC)

5.3.4.3 'People' display justifications

The least dominant theme was 'people'. Arguments within this theme typically acknowledged the potential for posters and flags to signal safe school environments. However, the support for posters and flags was conditional on the LGBTQ+-related school support being embedded within inclusive strategies afforded to other potential aspects of family diversity. Leximancer exemplary quotes of this theme included:

> The visible support would allow our children to feel a sense of belonging. The same as the Aboriginal flag being raised in the school, and multicultural posters and items being available assist people from those cultures to feel they belong at that school.
>
> (Madelyn, 42 yrs old, WA)

> It shows that LGBTQ+ people and families are welcome. Much like schools have families from diverse cultures.
>
> (Mark, 39 yrs old, VIC)

The themes identified by Leximancer thus indicated that LGBTQ+ related posters were a valued aspect of school Microsystems in signaling safe and inclusive school environments for LGBTQ+ parents and families. Although parents raised concerns about the relevance of such materials in creating meaningful change in school Microsystems, the potential for LGBTQ+ related iconography to be non-relatable to LGBTQ+ parented families and conditional support based on similar supportive features being offered to various forms of diversity including multiculturalism and a range of family structures.

5.3.5 Parents' perceptions of explicit mention of LGBTQ+ parents in school websites and documents

To explore participants' views of the LGBTQ+ related supports, parents were asked to respond to the open-ended question – 'Do you think it would be beneficial for your relationship to your child's school to include LGBTQ+-parented families in all brochures, websites and documents? Why or why not?'. Figure 5.4 displays Leximancer identified dominant themes through content analysis. Dominant themes included 'school' (46 Hits), 'feel' (20 Hits), 'inclusive' (18 Hits), 'kids' (5 Hits), 'sure' (4 Hits), 'types' (4 Hits) and 'people' (4 Hits).

5.3.5.1 'School' explicit mention justifications

The dominant theme 'school' highlights LGBTQ+ parents' endorsement of school websites and documents that explicitly mention LGBTQ+ families conditional on the inclusion of other forms of diversity. Leximancer exemplary quotes from the raw data highlighted:

> If there were brochures that included families, they should definitely include LGBTQ+ families. Our school doesn't really have any, so we're not being excluded from anything.
> (Drew, 40 yrs old, QLD)

> Inclusivity is important but again I would want websites/documents to include a diversity of families not just LGBTQ+.
> (Elisabeth, 37 yrs old, QLD)

> If a school provides information for parents on a variety of topics and issues then they should aim to make the material inclusive. To go one step further and include material, websites etc for specific community groups within the school is a sign of a thoughtful(ness)

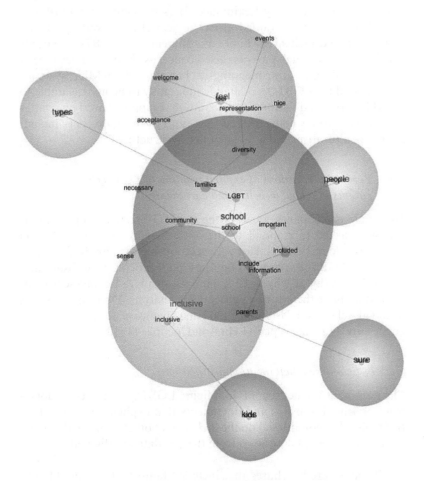

Figure 5.4 Leximancer map of parent's justifications for school websites and documents explicit mention LGBTQ+ families (*n* = 73).

that is being proactive in providing information to support all groups within the school. This would be very welcoming and would contribute to a sense of being wanted, catered for and accepted within the school community.

(Eloise, 52 yrs old, NSW)

5.3.5.2 'Feel' explicit mention justifications

The second dominant theme identified by Leximancer was 'feel'. This theme stressed how the explicit mention of LGBTQ+ parented families

in school websites and brochures could potentially encourage perceptions of safe/welcoming school environments and overcome parents'
concerns around disclosure in school contexts. Leximancer exemplary
quotes include:

> Maybe not "all" but definitely there should be representation.
> I would feel that showing this acceptance would mean that they
> were actively supporting future LGBTQ+ families who may have
> children at the school also.
>
> (Abbie, 40 yrs old, QLD)

> Visual representation of diverse families makes us feel safe, wel-
> come, and Supported.
>
> (Kennedy, 38 yrs old, QLD)

> I would then feel less threatened when bringing my wife to my
> daughter's special Events.
>
> (Abigail, 47 yrs old, NSW)

5.3.5.3 'People' explicit mention justifications

The least dominant and most distinct theme was 'people'. Leximancer
analysis of raw data highlighted the potential for the explicit mention
of LGBTQ+ parented families in school websites, brochures, and
documents to raise awareness and recognition of LGBTQ+ family
formations to school communities (parents, teachers and students).
Leximancer typical quotes included:

> … too many people live sheltered lives, they are not against LG-
> BTQ+ but are not even aware we exist, it would be nice to see some
> recognition.
>
> (Josephine, 43 yrs old, SA)

> LGBTQ+ people are part of society and schools and this should
> be represented in visual information. It promotes inclusivity and
> normalises LGBTQ+ families.
>
> (Monica, 36 yrs old, WA)

> It sets a clear guide on how schools can communicate about us.
> It tells the entire school community that we are represented and
> appreciated. If people don't want to be in this school that lists us
> specifically, they can find somewhere else.
>
> (Deborah, 37 yrs old, VIC)

The themes identified by Leximancer indicates that parents valued the explicit mention of LGBTQ+ families in school documents and websites in school Microsystems as a potential measure to raise awareness of various forms of family diversity in school communities, and potentially overcome parents' concerns around disclosure in school contexts. Although similar to previous themes in previous supports, parents often expressed conditional support based on the inclusion of other forms of family diversity.

5.3.6 Leximancer analysis of justifications for LGBTQ+ related lessons and books in school environments

Parent's perceptions of LGBTQ+ inclusive school curriculums were explored through participants' responses to the question 'Do you think lessons and books covering LGBTQ+ topics/issues would be beneficial to your experience of your child's school? Why or why not?'. The Leximancer map (Figure 5.5) and content analysis identified five dominant themes within responses including: 'families' (42 Hits),

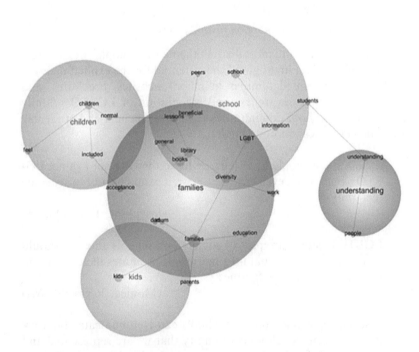

Figure 5.5 Leximancer map of LGBTQ+ parents' justifications for LGBTQ+ inclusive lessons and books in school Microsystems (*n* = 69).

'school' (32 Hits), 'children' (17 Hits), 'kids' (15 Hits) and 'understanding' (10 Hits). The following section discusses findings identified with 'families', 'school' and 'understanding' themes.

5.3.6.1 *'Families' lessons & books justifications*

The dominant theme identified by Leximancer was 'families'. The justifications identified for the inclusion of LGBTQ+ related lessons and books in this theme included the potential to normalise LGBTQ+ parented families as one of many types of family diversity, the potential to overcome concerns around exclusively heterosexual learning materials, and potential to endorse acceptance in school contexts. Leximancer identified typical quotes within this theme include:

I think lessons on family diversity in general which also included 2 mums or 2 dads as normal as well as single-parent families, multigenerational families, kids who live with other relatives or foster care etc and books which also reflect this family diversity would be beneficial for all children and our wider community.

(Gianna, 50 yrs, VIC)

Educational books and lessons specifically on LGBT information would likely be boring and may be divisive. Instead books that cover the diversity of families should be available in schools. If we stumble upon a book with 2 mums or 2 dads it lets my kids feel accepted. Books like "Just the way we are" talk about acceptance of all families. Some of our kids readers have had LGBT parents in them, divorced parents, culturally diverse it's a great way of normalizing difference. Some of the activities on families certainly needs some work. Our teachers have been great at altering activities to be more inclusive but there is still a lot of educational resources that have mum dad and two kids as the basis of the discussion. Inclusivity is the key when planning these types of education.

(Elisabeth, 37 yrs, QLD)

Our children live in a world of a mum and a dad (despite the family diversity that is within our schools and communities.) For them to have readers, see posters and library books that depict families similar to theirs helps to give a child a sense of belonging and a sense of acceptance.

(Eloise, 52 yrs, NSW)

5.3.6.2 'Schools' lessons & books justifications

The second dominant theme identified by Leximancer was 'schools'. Arguments included in this theme focussed on the benefits of LGBTQ+ inclusive curriculum in educating other school community members on diversity and removing the responsibility from children to educate others in family diversity. Leximancer extracted quotes from this theme include:

> Any information that can be provided to students about LGBTQ+ families is valuable in the sense that it provides education on a topic that isn't going to go away. It teaches diversity and tolerance of minority groups.
>
> (Renee, 54 yrs, NSW)

> Not beneficial as such, however would give other students an understanding of how the dynamics work for their fellow peers.
>
> (Cameron, 27 yrs, NSW)

> At the moment our children's peers are getting information from their homes only about same sex families and this is not always positive. Our children are having to address that themselves, which can lead to a feeling of isolation in the school yard.
>
> (Madelyn, 42 yrs, NSW)

5.3.6.3 'Understanding' lessons & books justifications

The most unique theme identified by Leximancer was 'understanding'. Arguments in this theme related to the benefits of an inclusive school curriculum in normalising LGBTQ+ parented families as one of many forms of family diversity and including positive representations of family diversity. Leximancer extracted quotes typical of this theme include:

> Visual indicators of safe spaces for LGBTQ+ people are vital. Plus it normalizes our families and gives positive talking points.
>
> (Laila, 47 yrs, NSW)

> I think it helps show there are all different types of families - and this has a positive impact for everyone in understanding we are the same, not different.
>
> (Mark, 39 yrs, VIC)

I think talking about it would provide more understanding and also shift that it is just another part of people. It's about inclusion and diversity.

(Yolanda, 38 yrs, QLD)

The themes identified by Leximancer thus indicated that lessons and books that cover LGBTQ+ topics and issues were a desired aspect of LGBTQ+ parent-school Microsystems. Justifications for inclusive curriculum materials and activities included normalising LGBTQ+ parented families as an acknowledged form of family diversity, educating school community members on family diversity within a positive framing, and addressing possible exclusion of LGBTQ+ parented families being represented within school environments.

5.4 Discussion

From the parents' perspectives, all of the LGBTQ+ related supportive features they were questioned about were deemed important and beneficial in creating welcoming school Microsystems. LGBTQ+ parents were unanimous in deeming teacher training and inclusive school forms as important and beneficial supportive features in creating welcoming school environments for LGBTQ+ parented families. Further, over 80% of the sample indicated all supportive features were important and beneficial in school environments including items that reflect LGBTQ+ families (posters and flags) followed by; LGBTQ+ families mentioned in documents/websites, LGBTQ+ inclusive school policies and LGBTQ+ inclusive curriculum (lessons and books). Notably, when viewed alongside the Australian Professional Standards of Teaching (AITSL, 2011) parents' preference for supportive structures reflected the importance of the parent-teacher interactions dictated by the national professional policy; teacher interpersonal interactions with parents and school-based communications (e.g. forms, newsletters). The difference in support for some features (e.g., teacher training 100%) over others (e.g., 80% inclusive curriculum) may be explained by the questioning adopted in this study. As this study sought to explore LGBTQ+ parent-school relationships, some parents could potentially discern between supports more relevant to parents and supports more beneficial for their children. The following section further explores the views of LGBTQ+ related supportive features in school contexts highlighting parent justifications for the inclusion of supportive; interpersonal characteristics (teacher competency in LGBTQ+ family structures and challenges), school procedures (LGBTQ+ inclusive school forms), materials (LGBTQ+ related posters and flags), school policies (explicit mention of LGBTQ+ parents in school documents and websites) and activities/resources (LGBTQ+ related lessons and books) in Australian school Microsystems.

5.4.1 Interpersonal characteristics within school Microsystems: teacher competency (training) in LGBTQ+ family structures

Interestingly, LGBTQ+ parents were highly uncertain whether teacher training in LGBTQ+ family structures was a component of their school Microsystems currently and yet, they deemed it one of the most beneficial and important supports in creating welcoming school environments. Parent justifications for teacher training in LG-BTQ+ topics included raising awareness of LGBTQ+ family structures within school communities, potentially normalising LGBTQ+ parented families as one of many forms of family diversity, making educators aware of the unique needs of LGBTQ+ parented children, and overcoming challenging parent-teacher social interactions. Consistent with previous research, challenging social interactions within this sample included instances where teachers lacked knowledge about LGBTQ+ forms of family diversity, teachers showed discomfort when discussing LGBTQ+ topics or issues, and parents were concerned about potential adverse reactions to themselves and their children when 'coming out' or disclosing their LGBTQ+ family structures to teachers (Casper et al., 1992; Goldberg et al., 2017; Goldberg & Smith, 2014a; Lindsay et al., 2006).

Leading arguments advocating the inclusion of teacher training in LGBTQ+ family structures as part of school Microsystems included; changing school climate (Goldberg, 2014) educating educators on diverse family constellations within classrooms (Riggs & Willing, 2013), addressing potential biases/stereotypes held by educators (Casper et al., 1992; Cloughessy et al., 2019) and developing sensitive practices to meet the needs of diverse families (Byard et al., 2013; Goldberg et al., 2017). International research has also found that LGBTQ+ parented families value 'Business-As-Usual' mindsets and pluralist views of family diversity, where LGBTQ+ parented families are offered the same treatment and accommodations as other families within school communities (Bower, 2008; Goldberg et al., 2017). Additionally, consistent with previous Australian and international research, this study indicates that not all LGBTQ+ parents are 'out' within school environments and list concerns of potential adverse reactions to disclosure of LGBTQ+ identity to school staff (Casper et al., 1992; Lindsay et al., 2006). From the perspective of LGBTQ+ parents, teacher training in LGBTQ+ topics and forms of family diversity may thus be a method of overcoming a range of unique barriers LGBTQ+ parents experience within school Microsystems, including gaps in teacher professional knowledge of family diversity and creating informed school communities for LGBTQ+ parented families' intended or unintended disclosures.

5.4.2 Procedural characteristics within school Microsystems: school forms inclusive of LGBTQ+ parented families

Within this sample, school forms and documents inclusive of LG-BTQ+ parented families were deemed equally as important as teacher training; and was the most common supportive structure (close to one-third) provided within LGBTQ+ parent-school Microsystems. From parents' perspective, dominant justifications for using inclusive forms in school Microsystems include school forms that accommodate all forms of family diversity, positioning diverse family structures as a 'non-issue' and a potential solution to exclusionary experiences with gendered language in school documents. Identified challenging experiences with school forms included the need to physically modify school forms to accommodate LGBTQ+ parented family structures and the negative/exclusionary effect of school documentation assuming dual-gendered heterosexual family formations. Thus, this Australian study echoed US research showing school forms were not accommodating diverse family structures (Casper et al., 1992; Goldberg, 2014). School forms that fail to acknowledge diverse family structures may act as 'first signals' to parents their families are not accommodated within social organisations and may be deemed 'other' in Microsystems (Casper et al., 1992). The frequency of school communications to parents further makes these reminders repetitive and the 'othering' process cumulative.

Similar to arguments for teacher training, the qualitative analysis of comments indicated LGBTQ+ parented families preferred school forms inclusive of all family structures, as opposed to specialised/differential additions *only* for LGBTQ+ parented families. This finding builds on US research previously arguing that LGBTQ+ parents positively assess school environments when family differences are treated equally with 'Business-As-Usual' mentalities (Goldberg et al., 2017).

Predominant arguments for the provision of school forms inclusive of diverse family structures include overcoming the potential devaluing of diverse family structures (Mercier & Harold, 2003), endorsing multiculturalism and anti-LGBTQ+ bias in schools (Casper et al., 1992) and creating pro-active environments that remove the onus placed on parents to advocate for the inclusion of their family structures (Goldberg, 2014). Consistent with international research, this study showed LGBTQ+ parents repeatedly modify forms to adequately accommodate their family structures, which has also been reported to confuse school staff in how to interpret the modifications and raise concerns in how to broach the topic with parents (Casper et al., 1992) This indicates that Australian school Microsystems commonly include procedures that fail to accommodate the diversity of family structures represented within school communities. It also highlights that LGBTQ+ parents may be required to interact with challenging materials and resources in school environments where parents must repeatedly physically modify forms to ensure their family structures 'fit' school documents.

5.4.3   *Material characteristics within school Microsystems:*
display of rainbow flags and posters that reflect
LGBTQ+ families within school contexts

LGBTQ+ related posters and flags were the second most common LGBTQ+ related support provided within school contexts (close to 20%) and were deemed both important and beneficial in creating welcoming school environments by an overwhelming majority of parents (96%). Although most parents supported the inclusion of LGBTQ+ related posters and flags in school contexts, parent justifications highlighted this support was conditional. Parent justifications for rainbow flags and posters depicting LGBTQ+ parented families in schools included increasing the representation and 'normalisation' of LGBTQ+ identities. Justifications also included signaling safe and welcoming school environments for LGBTQ+ parents and their children. However, parents indicated a range of concerns related to rainbow flags and posters. These included suspicions over their inability to create meaningful change in the treatment or views of LGBTQ+ identities in school contexts. Concerns related to rainbow flags included the lack of relevance of LGBTQ+ rainbow flag iconography to some families and conditional support of flags and posters when considering other forms of family and ethnic diversity (e.g., the need for Indigenous flags) rather than exclusive support of LGBTQ+ families.

The discrepant views of the benefit and usefulness of schools depicting LGBTQ+ related posters and flags in creating more welcoming environments for parents are reflected in previous research. School guide research advising strategies for creating welcoming school environments for LGBTQ+ parents and students commonly state the need for physical materials that reflect LGBTQ+ parents, students and families, including posters and flags (Fox, 2007). Similarly to parents' justifications, researchers argue that such objects are age-appropriate representations of LGBTQ+ forms of diversity that signal inclusivity, safety, and acknowledgement of LGBTQ+ family structures that are often excluded or marginalised in school contexts and materials (Bartholomaeus & Riggs, 2017; Duke & McCarthy, 2009; UNESCO, 2016).

However, parents' concerns around the benefits of LGBTQ+-related posters and flags have similarly been highlighted in previous research. Similar to parents' concerns around the inability of posters and flags to create meaningful change in school contexts, research exploring teacher perspectives has indicated LGBTQ+-related posters as tokenistic signs of support that are not actively engaged within teaching practices (Ferfolja, 2007). Additionally, research has found LGBTQ+ parents may not engage, relate, or have the support of the LGBTQ+ community, with some parents' identities and social networks shifting from predominantly LGBTQ+ related to parent and family-centric post-transition to parenthood (Perales et al., 2019). This may highlight the inappropriateness of exclusively LGBTQ+-related supports for parents.

Furthermore, parents' concerns around the inclusion of exclusive LGBTQ+ posters and flags are similar to previous research highlighting parents' value in school contexts that reflect, recognise and celebrate all forms of diversity (Bower, 2008; Goldberg & Smith, 2014a, 2014b). This theme of valuing various aspects of diversity including multiculturalism and other family formations is particularly strong in parent justifications for all supportive features in this study and is reflective of parents' desires for school environments to view LGBTQ+ parented families as one of many types of diversity present in school communities.

5.4.4 Policy characteristics within school Microsystems: explicit mention of LGBTQ+ families in school brochures, and documents

From the perspective of parents, explicit mention of LGBTQ+ families in school documents and websites was the second least important (86.3%) and beneficial (90.4%) supportive strategy in creating welcoming school environments. This supportive feature was deemed beneficial by parents in creating a sense of safety, acceptance and belonging for LGBTQ+ parents and their families. Explicit mention of LGBTQ+ families was also viewed as a method to inform school community members of the school's stance towards diversity and normalise LGBTQ+ parents as one of many forms of diversity in school communities. Aligning to parents' views of other supportive features, parent support was conditional on the basis of school websites and documents including LGBTQ+ parents alongside other minority groups and family formations. Parent justifications also indicated explicit mention of parents in school documents and websites could overcome parent concerns about potential reprisals to themselves and their families when 'coming out' or disclosing their family constellations to the school community.

Previous research has similarly argued the need for schools to explicitly include LGBTQ+ parented families in school websites, brochures and documents as a method to inform LGBTQ+ parents specifically they are included and represented within school environments (Fox, 2007; Lee, 2010; Ryan & Martin, 2000). It has also argued the need to inform the wider school community of a school's stance towards LGBTQ+ parented families (Casper et al., 1992; UNESCO, 2016). Also aligning with parent justifications provided in the study, guide research has argued such supportive features in school contexts may create more welcoming and inclusive school contexts and endorse open communication where parents and LGBTQ+ people broadly may feel less concerned about potential backlash, or lack of acceptance, upon disclosure of their family formations (Casper et al., 1992; Fox, 2007; Jones, 2015; Ryan & Martin, 2000). Additional positive aspects of the inclusion of LGBTQ+ parents in school websites and documents included the potential to justify other proactive forms of inclusivity; such as professional training for teachers in LGBTQ+ forms of family diversity and LGBTQ+ inclusive curriculums or learning activities (Ferfolja & Ullman, 2017; Flores, 2014).

5.4.5 Activity/material characteristics within school Microsystems: Inclusion of lessons and books on LGBTQ+ topics/issues within school contexts

The results indicated 'inclusive curriculum and books' was deemed the least important and least beneficial support for creating welcoming environments in schools. Nonetheless, over 80% of the sample indicated some importance and benefit. Additionally, curricula and books were the least likely supports to be offered within school Microsystems.

Indeed, over 60% of the sample indicated inclusive curricula were not components of their school contexts. Dominant themes identified within qualitative analysis indicated inclusive curriculum and books that reflect LGBTQ+ parented families were of benefit in school Microsystems in terms of; addressing concerns of over-representation of heterosexual parented families exclusively; raising awareness of LGBTQ+ topics/issues, tolerance and acceptance within school communities; embedding LGBTQ+ forms of the family as one of many forms of family diversity; and beneficial in raising awareness of child(ren)'s peers in family diversity to alleviate the onus placed on LGBTQ+ children to describe and justify their families.

Inclusive school curriculums and materials that reflect LGBTQ+ parented families have been argued to endorse consideration of multiculturalism (Casper et al., 1992), address the potential marginalisation of LGBTQ+ parented families in schools (Goldberg et al., 2017; Riggs & Willing, 2013) and are endorsed within the national curriculum where the inclusion of family/cultural backgrounds of students serve as familiar foundational experiences drawn on in learning environments (Australian Curriculum, Assessment and Reporting Authority/ACARA, 2019). The lack of inclusion of activities and resources reflecting LGBTQ+ parented families in this sample, lends support to sociological arguments that schools typically assume all families within schools are heterosexual and exclude 'other' diverse forms of the family (Casper et al., 1992; Goldberg et al., 2017; Rawsthorne, 2009). Through representing only one dominant form of family diversity, schools may contribute to the lack of awareness of LGBTQ+ parented family formations in school communities generally. Such lack of representation and knowledge of family diversity has been attributed to unique challenges experienced by LGBTQ+ parented children including misunderstandings between children, teachers, and other students; where it is up to children to advocate, explain and justify their family structures to others (Casper et al., 1992; Lindsay et al., 2006; Ray & Gregory, 2001). This sample's indication that LGBTQ+ parents value inclusive curriculums reflecting all forms of family diversity, rather than the exceptional inclusion of only one form of family structure diversity, also reflects previous international research (Bower, 2010; Goldberg et al., 2017).

Inclusive school activities and resources that reflect LGBTQ+ parented families (alongside other forms of family diversity) may aid in educating school communities and raise awareness about diverse forms of family, reduce difficulties experienced by LGBTQ+ parented children in school environments and address concerns of the predominance of schools reflecting traditional heterosexual family formations. However, the provision of LGBTQ+ inclusive curriculum and materials may prove problematic to some school systems given current debates and media coverage of LGBTQ+ identities being introduced to schools – most especially for Australia, the vicious nature of the public debate over the Safe Schools Coalition's curricula and resources such as Gayby Baby may have been an influential consideration (Ferfolja & Ullman, 2017; Law, 2017). Other LGBTQ+ parent books and other resources have also similarly been politicised by media (such as Heather Has Two Mummies in the UK). It is worth noting that the Safe Schools Coalition did not actually create or promote its own set curriculum in the traditional sense – this was a myth perpetuated by various journalists who knew little of the program other than its value in homophobic and transphobic dog whistles to conservative voters. The coalition was at its core (and mainly offered) a network, which distributed some resource documents with ideas for working on LGBTQ+ discrimination themes within or connecting to existing curricula priorities, commitments to such ideals as school-specific policy protections against and context ideas for the achievement of inclusive events and so forth. 'LGBTQ+ curricula' is a bogeyman in Australia, a figment accused of bizarre crimes like directly teaching students a how-to for 'penis-tucking' and other absurdities it was incapable of having committed, being that it didn't exist. However, the media's politicisation of curricula as phenomena within Macrosystems and Microsystems may have in part influenced the way LGBTQ+ parents (as Individuals within those systems) perceive its value and potential uses. This politicisation of curricula and resources may have also helped to shape their preference for the Business-As-Usual approach constructing LGBTQ+ people as a diversity like any other and not a sole focus for (potentially negative) attentions.

5.5 Summary of key points

Main ideas that were brought together here included:

- Parents were unanimous in perceiving interpersonal characteristics (teacher training in LGBTQ+ forms of family diversity) and procedural characteristics (LGBTQ+ inclusive school forms and documents) as important and beneficial in creating welcoming school environments.
- Over 80% of parents viewed all supportive features in Microsystems as important and beneficial in creating welcoming school

contexts, including materials (posters and flags), policies (explicit mention of LGBTQ+ parented families in websites/brochures), and activities (LGBTQ+ inclusive curriculums and books).

• Parents' justifications for the inclusion of supports were similar in raising awareness, acknowledgement, and recognition of LG-BTQ+ forms of family diversity in school contexts; overcoming challenging or marginalising experiences in school environments; endorsing perceptions of safe environments; and normalising LG-BTQ+ forms of family diversity as one of many forms of diversity in school settings.

• Parents' support of inclusive school features was highly provisional based on supports including LGBTQ+ parents alongside other forms of diversity and minority groups, rather than characteristics supportive of LGBTQ+ parents exclusively.

• Parents' strong but relatively lower support for LGBTQ+ curricula and books may relate to how these phenomena frequently feature in Australian (and international) media controversies; regardless of whether they are in actual use in schools or indeed, whether specific 'examples' under debate exist at all.

5.6 Conclusion & next chapter

This chapter highlighted how Australian LGBTQ+ parents particularly valued supports that reflected how they typically interact with school Microsystems, relations with teachers and school forms, over those historically made controversial like curricula and books – especially where they also included broader diversities. This reflected their multicultural context and worldviews, and also their concerns with having been overly politicised recently. The following chapter discusses LGBTQ+ parents' positive experiences and recommendations for schools.

References

ACARA. (2019). *Student Diversity*. Canberra: ACARA.

AITSL. (2011). *Australian Professional Standards for Teachers*. Canberra: AITSL.

Bartholomaeus, C., & Riggs, D. W. (2017). Whole-of-school approaches to supporting transgender students, staff, and parents. *The International Journal of Transgenderism, 18*(4), 361–366.

Bower, L. (2008). Standing up for diversity. *Kappa Delta Pi Record, 44*(4), 181–183.

Bower, L., & Klecka, C. (2009). (Re)considering normal. *Teaching Education, 20*(4), 357–373.

Braun, V., & Clarke, V. (2006). Using thematic analysis in psychology. *Qualitative Research in Psychology, 3*(2), 77–101.

Bronfenbrenner, U., & Crouter, A. (1983). The evolution of environmental models in developmental research. In P. Mussen & W. Kessen (Eds.), *Handbook of Child Psychology Volume 1* (pp. 357–414). New York: John Wiley.

Byard, E., Kosciw, J., & Bartkiewicz, M. (2013). *Schools and LGBT-parent families.* In A. E. Goldberg & K. R. Allen (Eds.), *LGBT-Parent Families* (pp. 275–290). New York: Springer.

Casper, V., Schultz, S., & Wickens, E. (1992). Breaking the silences. *Teachers College Record, 94*(1), 109–137.

Cloughessy, K., Waniganayake, M., & Blatterer, H. (2019). The good and the bad. *Journal of Research in Childhood Education, 33*(3), 446–458.

Duke, T. S., & McCarthy, K. W. (2009). Homophobia, sexism, and early childhood education. *Journal of Early Childhood Teacher Education, 30*(4), 385–403.

Ferfolja, T. (2007). Schooling cultures. *International Journal of Inclusive Education, 11*(2), 147–162.

Ferfolja, T., & Ullman, J. (2017). Gender and sexuality diversity and schooling. *Sex Education, 17*(3), 348–362.

Flores, G. (2014). Teachers working cooperatively with parents and caregivers when implementing LGBT themes in the elementary classroom. *American Journal of Sexuality Education, 9*(1), 114–120.

Fox, R. K. (2007). One of the hidden diversities in schools. *Childhood Education, 83*(5), 277–281.

Goldberg, A. E. (2014). Lesbian, gay, and heterosexual adoptive parents' experiences in preschool environments. *Early Childhood Research Quarterly, 29*(4), 669–681.

Goldberg, A. E., Black, K., Sweeney, K., & Moyer, A. (2017). Lesbian, gay, and heterosexual adoptive parents' perceptions of inclusivity and receptiveness in early childhood education settings. *Journal of Research in Childhood Education, 31*(1), 141–159.

Goldberg, A. E., & Smith, J. Z. (2014a). Perceptions of stigma and self-reported school engagement in same-sex couples with young children. *Psychology of Sexual Orientation and Gender Diversity, 1*(3), 202–212.

Goldberg, A. E., & Smith, J. Z. (2014b). Preschool selection considerations and experiences of school mistreatment among lesbian, gay, and heterosexual adoptive parents. *Early Childhood Research Quarterly, 29*(1), 64–75.

Herbstrith, J. C., & Busse, G. A. (2020). Seven million and counting. *Journal of Educational and Psychological Consultation, 30*(1), 29–62.

Jones, T. (2015). *Policy and Gay, Lesbian, Bisexual, Transgender and Intersex Students.* New York: Springer.

Law, B. (2017). Moral panic 101. *Quarterly Essay, 67,* 1–80.

Lee, D. (2010). Gay mothers and early childhood education. *Australasian Journal of Early Childhood, 35*(1), 16–23.

Leland, A. S. (2017). Navigating gay fatherhood. *Gender and Education, 29*(5), 632–647.

Lindsay, J., Perlesz, A., Brown, R., McNair, R., De Vaus, D., & Pitts, M. (2006). Stigma or respect. *Sociology, 40*(6), 1059–1077.

Mercier, L., & Harold, R. (2003). At the interface. *Children & Schools, 1,* 35–47.

Perales, F., Simpson Reeves, L., Plage, S., & Baxter, J. (2019). The family lives of Australian lesbian, gay and bisexual people. *Sexuality Research & Social Policy, 17*(1), 43–60.

Rawsthorne, M. L. (2009). Just like other families? *Australian Social Work, 62*(1), 45–60.

Riggs, D. W., & Willing, I. (2013). "They're all just little bits, aren't they". *Journal of Australian Studies, 37*(3), 364–377.

Robinson, K. H. (2002). Making the invisible visible. *Contemporary Issues in Early Childhood, 3*(3), 415–434.

Ryan, D., & Martin, A. (2000). Lesbian, gay, bisexual, and transgender parents in the school systems. *School Psychology Review, 29*(2), 207–216.

UNESCO. (2016). *Out In The Open.* Paris: UNESCO.

6 Emphasising LGBTQ+ parents' positive experiences in, & recommendations for, school contexts

LGBTQ+ parents reflect on: acceptance & inclusion

I have had acceptance and welcome, consistently at our child's school. Any awkwardness, such as getting mine and my partner's name switched, has been dealt with openly and with good humour. We are both involved in reading with the children in the same younger class, which has formed a focus around our children, who identify us as "the two mums". When we initially contacted the school to see about enrolment, we were told by the Principal that our family would be "a blessing" in the school. Staff have checked things with us from time to time, to make sure we are travelling ok.

(Fran, 48 yrs, SA)

Mine are only in primary and daycare so it's still pretty simple. Just stories about different families and transgender kids is really all they need at the moment.

(Beatrice, 39 yrs, QLD)

History curriculum in prep covers different families.

(Elle, 44 yrs, QLD)

Individual teachers have been great. When my son was in kindergarten they were looking at the 7 wonders of the world. He was telling the teacher that his mums had been to some of the wonders. The teacher purposely asked him, 'was that just one of your mums or both of them?'

(Eloise, 52 yrs, NSW)

6.1 Introduction: taking LGBTQ+ parents' perspectives

The previous chapter explored LGBTQ+ parents' views of supportive features commonly endorsed by LGBTQ+ research, namely teacher training in LGBTQ+ family structures, LGBTQ+ inclusive forms,

DOI: 10.4324/9781003167471-6

mention of LGBTQ+ parents in school websites and documents, and LGBTQ+ inclusive curriculums. However, as these supports were driven by previous research (e.g. Ryan & Martin, 2000), it may limit participants' opportunities to highlight other important and valuable supportive characteristics. Researchers have similarly argued the need for empirical evidence drawn from the perspective of LGBTQ+ parents to inform the development of inclusive school policy (Liang & Cohrssen, 2020; Rawsthorne, 2009; Ullman & Ferfolja, 2016; Vaughan & Rodriguez, 2014).

6.2 Parents' positive experiences in school environments

The majority of LGBTQ+ parents indicate their relationships with their child's school are positive (Cloughessy et al., 2019; Goldberg & Smith, 2014a; Rawsthorne, 2009). Early research tended to explore challenging experiences in school contexts such as perceptions of stigma (Goldberg & Smith, 2014a), potential experiences of being excluded within school contexts (Kosciw & Diaz, 2008), and challenges with coming out or disclosing identification as LGBTQ+ parents to school personnel (Casper et al., 1992). More recent research has begun to explore more affirmative and positive experiences in school contexts for both parents and youth to counter victimisation narratives for LGBTQ+ people (Goldberg et al., 2017; Jones et al., 2016). Some have balanced approaches exploring both strengths and barriers posed by schools for LGBTQ+ parents (Cloughessy et al., 2019; Leland, 2017). This shift in research may also be explained in part by increasingly affirmative changes in Exosystems such as greater legal and societal protections, and acknowledgement/ recognition in most countries that privilege this type of research. Generally, this research has found that LGBTQ+ parents do not commonly experience overt forms of discrimination in school contexts but do experience covert forms of marginalisation and exclusion through policies, procedures and practices highlighted in the previous chapter.

Research exploring LGBTQ+ parents' positive experiences in schools has found LGBTQ+ parents value teachers who are collaborative with parents in creating welcoming school environments, teachers who develop LGBTQ+ inclusive learning environments acknowledging various points of diversity, educators who employ culturally sensitive teaching practices (e.g. non-gendered language, inclusive learning activities) and school environments that treat LGBTQ+ forms of family diversity as just another aspect of diversity or a non-issue (Bower, 2008; Cloughessy et al., 2019; Goldberg, 2014; Goldberg et al., 2017). Yet, the majority of research exploring parent positive experiences in schools has been drawn from Early Childhood educational contexts (Cloughessy et al., 2018, 2019; Goldberg et al., 2017; Goldberg & Smith, 2014a, 2014b), with little research exploring the positive experiences of parents in other educational environments.

This small but growing body of research adopting a positive lens to research, and offering parents the opportunity to put forward their own valued experiences in school contexts is important as the majority of suggestions for improving schools have come from researchers and inclusive guide literature (e.g. Fox, 2007; Goldberg, 2014; Ryan & Martin, 2000 and others) which may overlook the perspective of the minority group such supports are intended to serve. Educational policy guidelines such as the Professional Standards of Teaching (Australian Institute for Teaching and School Leadership/AITSL, 2011) and research (Bartholomaeus & Riggs, 2017; Liang & Cohrssen, 2020) similarly argue the need for schools to include the perspective of representatives of minority groups in exploring the needs and development of LGBTQ+ inclusive school policies, procedures and practices. As a result, this study explored LGBTQ+ parents' positive experiences and recommendations for creating welcoming school environments as a method to privilege the voices of an under-represented minority group in developing LGBTQ+ inclusive school contexts (Vaughan & Rodriguez, 2014). The following section highlights the findings from qualitative and quantitative analysis exploring parents' positive experiences in school Microsystems (Section 6.2.1), parents' recommendations for creating more welcoming school Microsystems (Section 6.2.2) and a discussion of the results with previous research (Section 6.3).

6.2.1 Parents' positive experiences in school Microsystems

Quantitative analysis of parent responses indicated most parents (69.86%) had positive experiences in school Microsystems, although close to 25% of the sample indicated a simple no response, as highlighted in Table 6.1.

Positive experiences in school contexts were explored by asking participants 'Have you had any positive experiences with your child's

Table 6.1 LGBTQ+ Parent Response Rate to Positive Experiences in Schools (*n* = 73)

	Response Rate		
Questions	Yes	No	Missing
Positive experiences	51	17	5

school or teacher as an LGBTQ+ parent? Please explain/give examples'. Qualitative analysis via Leximancer identified dominant themes: 'school' (45 Hits), 'teachers' (29 Hits), 'positive' (22 Hits), 'mums' (15 Hits) and 'plebiscite' (7 Hits). The Leximancer concept map is highlighted in Figure 6.1. The following section discusses exemplary quotes identified within the themes of 'school', 'teachers' and 'plebiscite'.

6.2.1.1 'School' positive experiences

The dominant theme identified by Leximancer was 'school'. This theme indicated that LGBTQ+ parents valued school environments where their family constellations were acknowledged, accepted, and accommodated within school practices. Exemplary quotes identified by Leximancer particularly highlight the positive perceptions of equal treatment of all forms of family diversity. Examples include:

> Perceived benefits of school educators/personnel being accepting, tolerant and treated/recognised as any other school type –

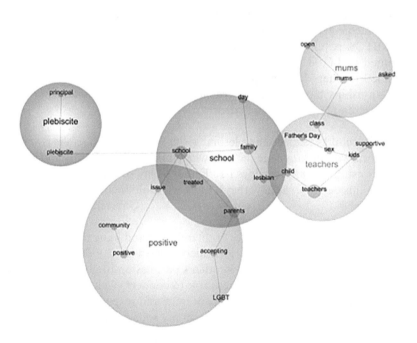

Figure 6.1 Leximancer analysis of LGBTQ+ parents' positive experiences within school Microsystems ($n = 51$).

accepted as simply one form of family diversity represented within school communities – thus 'normal'.

(Ciara, 38 yrs, Vic)

At our intake interview our daughters whole family was welcomed this included lesbian mum, transparent and her two dads....was just a non-issue.

(Luna, 51 yrs, NSW)

Our sons school has treated us as any other family. The school is very warm and welcoming of us. The teachers have always treated both myself and my wife as equal parents.

(Irene, 37 yrs, NSW)

We are not treated any differently by the teachers at our school. They are always accommodating around Mother's day and Father's Day.

(Karen, 43 yrs, VIC)

6.2.1.2 *'Teachers' positive experiences*

The second dominant theme identified by Leximancer was 'teachers'. This theme highlights different aspects of school personnel valued by LGBTQ+ parents. Educational employee characteristics particularly valued by LGBTQ+ parents highlighted in participant responses included teachers knowledgeable about family diversity, collaborative relationships between parent-teachers, and inclusive teaching practices. Exemplary quotes included:

Our child's teacher has a lesbian sister with kids and so she is very aware of the language she uses when talking about family and also consultative around days like Father's Day so that kids with two mums can discuss how they'd like their child included.

(Gabriella, 49 yrs, WA)

Had all kids draw pictures of their family and hang them on wall. At day-care, the teacher identified there were 2 kids from same sex families and asked each other's permission to give each other our contact details so we were able to connect. Went out of way to make 2 of every Mother's Day present and respected our request to call Father's Day, family day on my sons cards and make presents for his siblings as well.

(Beatrice, 39 yrs, QLD)

... teacher talks openly to the child and class about two mother families.

(Samantha, 42 yrs, VIC)

6.2.1.3 *'Plebiscite' positive experiences*

The least dominant theme identified by Leximancer was 'plebiscite'. This theme highlighted instances where schools acknowledged the potential harm of political debate during the marriage equality postal survey (plebiscite) and adopted pro-active supportive strategies. Leximancer exemplary quotes of this theme include, Sally (37 yrs, SA) stated *'during the plebiscite the principal several times checked in with us to see how we were travelling and if we were being too badly impacted, which was just lovely'*, Ivy (39 yrs, VIC) noted *'The school chaplain released a lovely article to parents during the plebiscite to support the local LGBTQ+ community which was nice'*, and Jacob (49 yrs, VIC) responded *'Lots of support during the marriage equality plebiscite. Lots of support and questions in discussing our son's 2 dad family'*.

The concepts identified by Leximancer centered on welcoming school environments, including LGBTQ+ parents being treated as a legitimate form of family or non-issue, flexibility on family celebratory days associated with 'traditional' heterosexual parented families, inclusive language use by educators, collaborative flexible teaching practices and proactive supportive messages from schools during highly political climates.

6.2.2 *Parents' recommendations for improving school contexts*

As this study adopted a positive psychological framing (Vaughan & Rodriguez, 2014), a key component of the research aimed to explore LGBTQ+ parents' suggestions on how to create more welcoming school environments. To explore LGBTQ+ parents' recommendations for supportive school improvements, participants were asked to respond to the open-ended item 'Please list any suggestions you have for schools or teachers, in terms of making LGBTQ+ parented families feel more welcome in your child's school community'. Most of the sample responded (71.23%) offering suggestions on how schools could be more welcoming of LGBTQ+ parented families. The Leximancer map (Figure 6.2) and content analysis of responses identified seven dominant themes: 'families (34 Hits). 'kids (30 Hits), 'inclusive' (22 Hits), 'school' (21 Hits), 'day' (18 Hits), LGBTQ+ (13 Hits) and education (Six

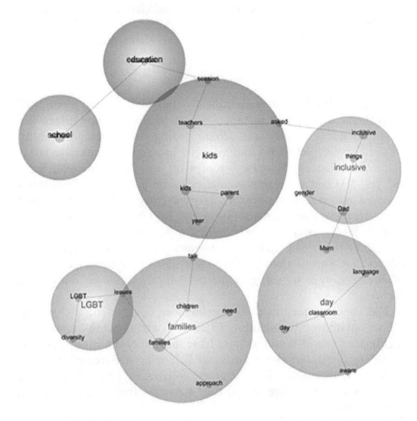

Figure 6.2 Leximancer analysis of LGBTQ+ parents' suggestions for creating welcoming environments in schools (*n* = 52).

Hits). The following section discusses the exemplary quotes of 'families', 'kids' and 'education'.

6.2.2.1 *'Families' improvement suggestions*

Leximancer identified 'families' as the dominant theme within LG-BTQ+ parent responses. Suggestions within this theme were practical approaches for schools to be more inclusive including careful language use, inclusive teaching practices to normalise LGBTQ+ parented families and inclusion of LGBTQ+ parented families within bullying policies. Leximancer identified extracts typical of this theme highlight various aspects of inclusive school environments desired within school environments. These concepts included:

> Teachers need to be aware of language used in classrooms and on notes. Ensure that all children are taught that all family structures are ok and there is nothing wrong with not having a Dad or not having a Mum for example. Mothers Day and Fathers Day need to be more inclusive of different types of families ... just say things like you are special to me or I love you is heaps better then saying "best Dad" and then getting kids who don't have a dad to have to add the word "grand" in front of Dad so they can give it to their grandfather. My eldest daughter ... experienced many bad experiences at school with regards to things like this. Thankfully my youngest ...has not had as many bad experiences but the school still has a long way to go.
>
> (Gianna, 50 yrs, VIC)

> Generally, be aware and be inclusive. Include LGBTQ+ families in your range of story books. Talk about all types of families. Have a zero tolerance approach to bullying / teasing of any kind. Asking families for their preferences, when appropriate (eg, leading up to Mothers Day 'Am I correct that XXXX has 2 mums? Great, just checking as we'll be making our mother's day flower crafts next week.)
>
> (Cora, 32 yrs, SA)

> Acknowledging the family dynamic and understanding the extra support needed for LGBTQ+ children families...eg bullying due to a child being from a LGBTQ+ family.
>
> (Renee, 54 yrs, NSW)

6.2.2.2 'Kids' improvement suggestions

The second dominant theme was 'kids'. This theme included suggestions for schools and teachers to be more aware and knowledgeable of LGBTQ+ forms of family diversity to overcome potential points of exclusion of children in schools. Leximancer identified exemplary quotes in this theme included:

> The problem is mostly that it's patchy. They try hard but then there'll be a form that lists mother and father. Or an announcement that kids can buy two presents at the mother's day stall

'for Mum and Grandma' which is unnecessarily not inclusive. A section in the curriculum on 'ancestry' caused some problems because the teacher just hadn't thought through what that looked like for kids living with one or more non-genetic parents. They were receptive but a little naive. Teachers are constantly saying things like 'Give it to your Mum and Dad' or 'get your Mum and Dad to help you'. This excludes all kinds of families. It's not deliberate but it does get frustrating. One day, a teacher asked 'Hands up if you do chores for your Mum and Dad'. Our youngest kept her hand down - not because she doesn't do chores but because she thought they were asking if she had a 'Mum and Dad'. So it causes unnecessary confusion sometimes and our kids get fed up with it. And that's in a supportive school. Forms also always ask if the kids are male or female, or ask the kids to line up according to whether they are boys or girls. This irritates us because it isn't inclusive, even though our kids are cis (as far as we know). Most teachers haven't figured out the two mums thing yet, let alone the complexities of gender and identity.

(Drew, 40 yrs, QLD)

Just more understanding from outsiders who generalize and have misconceptions of family. One incident with a teacher which upset our child would have been avoided if they asked our child for an explanation.

(Paige, 41 yrs, NT)

I would love it if there was an opportunity to have a face to face interview with a teacher before the school year starts just to demystify our family situation so they can start their relationship with our kids with some knowledge of where they come from (rather than assumptions made from an education session). I believe that would be helpful for all families. Don't single out LGBTQ+ families for this, that again just makes it seem like we need to explain ourselves. Make that connection early and help facilitate understanding.

(Elizabeth, 37 yrs, QLD)

6.2.2.3 'School' improvement suggestions

The least dominant theme identified by Leximancer was 'school'. Suggestions identified within this theme highlighted how schools may differ in the provision of LGBTQ+-related school supports and their stances toward diversity. Generally, this theme highlighted LGBTQ+ parents' satisfaction with schools that were adequately supportive of their forms of family. Leximancer identified exemplary quotes of this theme included:

> We are so welcome at our school there isn't anything I would change in that way.
>
> (Brittany, 47 yrs, VIC)

> All schools should be like ours. Safe schools will help.
>
> (Samantha, 42 yrs, VIC)

The themes identified within LGBTQ+ parents' suggestions for creating welcoming school Microsystems included; raising awareness and knowledge of LGBTQ+ parented families in school environments to overcome misconceptions, appropriately inclusive teaching practices to overcome potential points of exclusion of LGBTQ+ parented children, normalising LGBTQ+ family formations as part of normal family diversity in school communities, bullying policy explicitly including LGBTQ+ parented families and little suggestion for improvement when parents were satisfied with provision of school supportive features.

6.3 Discussion

In terms of positive experiences in schools, close to 70% of LGBTQ+ parents in this study had positive experiences within their child(ren)'s school Microsystem. Dominant themes identified in responses included experiences where; LGBTQ+ family diversity was treated as a non-issue, inclusive practices from teachers particularly during traditional family celebratory days (such as Mother's Day and Father's Day) and supportive messages from school community personnel during the plebiscite (a postal survey measuring national support for the legalisation of marriage equality). Previous research has similarly found LGBTQ+ parents value 'Business-As-Usual' mentalities where schools offer equal treatment regardless of family structures (Goldberg et al., 2017) and collaboratively differentiating lessons on traditional family centric celebratory days to accommodate LGBTQ+ family structures (Cloughessy et al., 2018; Goldberg, 2014).

Thus, this study underscored previous research arguing that LGBTQ+ parents see their family structures being treated equally and similarly to other forms of family diversity as 'positive' (Bower,

2008; Goldberg et al., 2017). Affirming the positivity of placing LG-BTQ+ parented families within and amongst other forms of diversity was heavily stressed by respondents throughout this study, where LG-BTQ+ parents deem supportive structures as beneficial conditional on the inclusion of all forms of family diversity. This may possibly indicate LGBTQ+ parents desire more mainstream recognition but also may indicate an ideological commitment to pluralism within school Microsystems.

The findings of schools offering support during the marriage equality survey highlight the differential stance and provision of supports across school Microsystems, and how some support types are only temporarily important, conditional on changing facets of Exo- and Chronosystems. The evident pro-actively supportive stance of some schools during the plebiscite in 2017 indicates some school environments deemed hostile political climates as potentially significant in school community members' individual development and made attempts to address possible negative impacts, similar to recommendations in research exploring the influence of mass media on the mental health of LGBTQ+ community members (Knight et al., 2017). Further research is needed to explore what school characteristics are related to more progressive/inclusionary or conservative/exclusionary school engagements with exosystem (e.g. political debates) and microsystem (e.g. inclusive curriculum) components. Additionally, further research may be needed to explore challenging experiences within school Microsystems as close to 30% of the sample indicated no positive events within schools.

As this study explored LGBTQ+ parents' perspectives on commonly endorsed supportive school structures, it became imperative to explore what supportive structures LGBTQ+ parented families may encourage and value not already captured within research. Thematic analysis of 52 responses identified dominant typical suggestions for school improvements included; suggestions for teachers to be mindful of language and activities that may potentially exclude their children, knowledge and awareness of different facets of family diversity in teachers to challenge stereotypes or misconceptions, educating all school community members of family diversity and endorse tolerance/acceptance within school contexts, the specific inclusion of LGBTQ+ parented families within bullying policy/supports and lack of suggestions for schools when LGBTQ+ parents' needs are adequately met. The findings relating to LGBTQ+ parented families suggesting schools be mindful of inclusive practices and stereotypes of LGBTQ+ parents and their children are congruent with previous research finding school staff may hold negative stereotypical beliefs or employ language that may inadvertently exclude children parented by LGBTQ+ identities (Casper et al., 1992; Lindsay et al., 2006). Arguably, the samples' predominant arguments on suggestions for schools could be categorised as teacher training in LGBTQ+ parented families, as inclusive language, awareness of family diversity and differentiation of school activities to accommodate LGBTQ+ parented children may be incorporated within pedagogical approaches and inclusive practices respectful of diversity.

The suggestions relating to more supportive structures centered on bullying warrants further research. Previous research has indicated LGBTQ+ parented children are no more likely to be teased within schools, but are more likely to be bullied regarding LGBTQ+ issues (Ray & Gregory, 2001; Tasker, 2005). However, this research is somewhat dated and may not report LGBTQ+ parented child(ren)'s experiences today. LGBTQ+ parents have been notedly concerned about isolation, bullying and adverse social contexts for their children (Casper et al., 1992; Rawsthorne, 2009), yet few contemporary studies (particularly in Australian samples) have explored the frequency, rate or nature of challenging social contexts for the children of LGBTQ+ parents. The findings that some parents were satisfied with their school environments and had no suggestions for improving school Microsystems highlights the differential provision of supportive structures within schools and LGBTQ+ parents' 'positivity' in 'Business-As-Usual' mentalities (Goldberg, 2014; Goldberg et al., 2017).

6.4 Summary of key points

From the perspective of parents, positive characteristics in schools include:

- School contexts that treat LGBTQ+ parents as mainstream recognised and accepted forms of family diversity.
- School staff who:
  - are knowledgeable and accepting of LGBTQ+ forms of family diversity,
  - adopt inclusive teaching practices in classroom environments such as open discussions around LGBTQ+ forms of family diversity, use of non-gendered language, include representation of LGBTQ+ forms of family diversity in classrooms environments,
  - developed quality parent-teacher relationships and reached out to parents during family centric activities.

- School environments that acted as a potential formal and informal source of support during challenging political environments (same-sex marriage debate).

Parent suggestions for creating welcoming school environments include;

- Schools that include representation of LGBTQ+ parented families and frame these family constellations as one of many forms of family diversity,
- Teaching staff and school communities that are knowledgeable, aware, and tolerant of LGBTQ+ forms of family diversity, and employ practical pedagogical knowledge to accommodate potential points of exclusion or needs for differentiation.
- Teachers and schools that build strong collaborative parent-teacher relationships.
- Explicit mention of LGBTQ+ parented families within school anti-bullying policy.

6.5 Conclusion & next chapter

This chapter showed parents value and desire teachers who are knowledgeable of different forms of family and competent in developing learning environments that are inclusive through practical teaching practices such as non-gendered language, adapted family-centric learning activities and acknowledgement and awareness of LGBTQ+ families in school communities. The next chapter offers the implications of the study for a range of educational stakeholders and recommendations for future research.

References

AITSL. (2011). *Australian Professional Standards for Teachers*. Canberra: AITSL.

Bartholomaeus, C., & Riggs, D. W. (2017). Whole-of-school approaches to supporting transgender students, staff, and parents. *The International Journal of Transgenderism, 18*(4), 361–366.

Bower, L. (2008). Standing up for diversity. *Kappa Delta Pi Record, 44*(4), 181–183.

Casper, V., Schultz, S., & Wickens, E. (1992). Breaking the silences. *Teachers College Record, 94*(1), 109–137.

Cloughessy, K., Waniganayake, M., & Blatterer, H. (2018). This is our family. We do not hide who we are. *Journal of GLBT Family Studies, 14*(4), 381–399.

Cloughessy, K., Waniganayake, M., & Blatterer, H. (2019). The good and the bad. *Journal of Research in Childhood Education, 33*(3), 446–458.

Fox, R. K. (2007). One of the hidden diversities in schools. *Childhood Education, 83*(5), 277–281.

Goldberg, A. E. (2014). Lesbian, gay, and heterosexual adoptive parents' experiences in preschool environments. *Early Childhood Research Quarterly, 29*(4), 669–681.

Goldberg, A. E., Black, K., Sweeney, K., & Moyer, A. (2017). Lesbian, gay, and heterosexual adoptive parents' perceptions of inclusivity and receptiveness in early childhood education settings. *Journal of Research in Childhood Education, 31*(1), 141–159.

Goldberg, A. E., & Smith, J. Z. (2014a). Perceptions of stigma and self-reported school engagement in same-sex couples with young children. *Psychology of Sexual Orientation and Gender Diversity, 1*(3), 202–212.

Goldberg, A. E., & Smith, J. Z. (2014b). Preschool selection considerations and experiences of school mistreatment among lesbian, gay, and heterosexual adoptive parents. *Early Childhood Research Quarterly, 29*(1), 64–75.

Jones, T., Smith, E., Ward, R., Dixon, J., Hillier, L., & Mitchell, A. (2016). School experiences of transgender and gender diverse students in Australia. *Sex Education, 16*(2), 156–171.

Knight, K. W., Stephenson, S. E., West, S., Delatycki, M. B., Jones, C. A., Little, M. H., Patton, G. C., Sawyer, S. M., Skinner, S. R., Telfer, M. M., Wake, M., North, K. N., & Oberklaid, F. (2017). The kids are OK. *Medical Journal of Australia, 207*(9), 374–375.

Kosciw, J. G., & Diaz, E. M. (2008). *Involved, Invisible, Ignored.* New York: GLSEN.

Leland, A. S. (2017). Navigating gay fatherhood. *Gender and Education, 29*(5), 632–647.

Liang, X., & Cohrssen, C. (2020). Towards creating inclusive environments for LGBTIQ-parented families in early childhood education and care settings. *Australasian Journal of Early Childhood, 45*(1), 43–55.

Rawsthorne, M. L. (2009). Just like other families? *Australian Social Work, 62*(1), 45–60.

Ray, V., & Gregory, R. (2001). School experiences of the lesbian and gay. *Family Matters, 59*, 28–34.

Ryan, D., & Martin, A. (2000). Lesbian, gay, bisexual, and transgender parents in the school systems. *School Psychology Review, 29*(2), 207–216.

Tasker, F. (2005). Lesbian mothers, gay fathers, and their children. *Journal of Developmental and Behavioral Pediatrics, 26*(3), 224–240.

Ullman, J., & Ferfolja, T. (2016). The elephant in the (class) room. *The Australian Journal of Teacher Education, 41*(10), 15–29.

Vaughan, M. D., & Rodriguez, E. M. (2014). LGBT strengths. *Psychology of Sexual Orientation and Gender Diversity, 1*(4), 325–334.

7 Summary and conclusions

Endorsing low-fuss pluralistic business-as-usual inclusion

LGBTQ+ parents reflect on: schools & pluralist family diversities
School motto reflects and celebrates diversity. Diversity is bigger than LGBTIQ and it's the intersectionality that is important. The school promotes diversity and inclusion of all. The school doesn't 'celebrate' Mother's day, Easter or Xmas so no issues at all.

(Luna, 51 yrs, New South Wales)

We received Mother's day gifts and crafts for dad and that we do things mum do in other families. The same is done for 2 mum and solo mums on fathers day. These mums are great and do things other dads do.

(Tom, 49 yrs, Queensland)

We are included as parents/guardians of our son like all parents. It is generic in one sense which is inclusive by result.

(Jacob, 49 yrs, Victoria)

It would be nice to see some books about diverse families on the bookshelf though. I check every week and have never seen anything.

(Clarissa, 36 yrs, Queensland)

7.1 Introduction: reflections on what was learned

The previous chapters have discussed LGBTQ+ views on 'if and how' LGBTQ+ parents should be approached, included and discussed in their children's school environments – including providing real-world examples of 'what worked'. This chapter reflects on dominant themes identified in the study, and how it relates to previous research and suggestions for schools. It discusses 'how' LGBTQ+ parents would like to be included in schools in a variety of ways, including their perspectives on specific supports such as teacher training in LGBTQ+ topics

DOI: 10.4324/9781003167471-7

or issues and inclusive school enrolment forms. The chapter outlines LGBTQ+ parents' ideal model of inclusion, and some issues around its geographic transferability and historical factors affecting its composition. The chapter continues with implications for policymakers and politicians, university teacher educators, schools, educational professionals, and researchers. The chapter concludes with a summary of key points in this publication and recommendations for future policy endeavours.

7.2 Affirming schools rare, even when searched for in affirming lenses

Based on the Australian study, this book reported on utilised positive psychology (Vaughan et al., 2014) and social-psychological frameworks (Bronfenbrenner & Crouter, 1986) to explore 'if and how' LGBTQ+ parents would like to be included in Australian school policy, procedures and practices. To do this, the study sought to find out how often LGBTQ+ inclusive school supports were provided by Australian schools, how LGBTQ+ parents framed their perceived benefit and importance, and how LGBTQ+ parents justified such supports. Information gleaned from the study on the perceived importance, benefit, provision and dominant justifications for each of the school supports considered according to LGBTQ+ parents is collated in Table 7.1. Comparing this information altogether exposes how LGBTQ+ parents saw the benefit of school supports, as having a relationship to their importance. Supports considered more beneficial in creating welcoming school contexts (particularly teacher training, and inclusive school forms and communications) were of more import to LGBTQ+ parents. LGBTQ+ parents were more likely to report inclusive forms and communications were used in schools, were most likely to report curricula and resources were *not used*, and that they were unclear on the occurrence of teacher training.

The study found, consistent with previous arguments in research, that LGBTQ+ forms of family diversity were not commonly explicitly included or accommodated within Australian school-level policies, practices and procedures (Fox, 2007). Important conclusions to be drawn from the study include that overall, like US samples, Australian LGBTQ+ parented families desire and value being included within a pluralistic 'Business-As-Usual' model of diversity (Goldberg et al., 2017). Parent justifications for the inclusion of supportive features within school contexts were commonly conditional on the supports including all different types of family structures rather than school

Table 7.1 LGBTQ+ Parents' Perceptions and Awareness of Different Supports in LGBTQ+ Inclusive School Strategies.

Support	Parent Perceptions of Support in Creating Welcoming School Contexts		Parent Awareness of Support in Schools		
	% of LGBTQ+ parents call it important	% of LGBTQ+ parents call it beneficial	% of LGBTQ+ parents say 'Yes' it occurs	% of LGBTQ+ parents say 'No' it does not	% of LGBTQ+ parents 'Unsure'
Teacher training in LGBTQ+ families	100.0	100.0	12.3	26.3	61.4

Justifications:

- Overcome LGBTQ+ parents' concerns of potential backlash to disclosure by others in schools.
- Address commonly held misconceptions and identified knowledge gaps in educational professionals and other members of school communities (other parents and students).
- Useful in acknowledging and supporting all school community members who may potentially identify as LGBTQ+ (e.g., other parents, students, children, teachers).
- Value educational staff members who know how to adapt teaching practices (such as gendered language use) and lessons on families to be inclusive of parents that may not have mothers, fathers, or strictly follow biological or legal definitions of families.
- Creates more welcoming school environments by raising awareness of, and appropriate responses to LGBTQ+ identities generally.

Support	% of LGBTQ+ parents call it important	% of LGBTQ+ parents call it beneficial	% of LGBTQ+ parents say 'Yes' it occurs	% of LGBTQ+ parents say 'No' it does not	% of LGBTQ+ parents 'Unsure'
Inclusive school forms and communications	100	100	27.83	50.43	21.74

Justifications:

- Overcomes parents having to manually change school forms to be inclusive of their families (e.g., crossing out Mother, Father and other gendered titles).
- Overcomes parents' feelings of being excluded in routine school communications that only mention Mothers and Fathers.
- Adapt forms to allow families to disclose their structures focussing on their relationships to the student (e.g., parent/carer/guardian, or empty spaces) that can include two or more active parents.
- Overall satisfaction when conducted in a generic way that accommodates all forms of family structures.

	% of LGBTQ+ parents call it important	% of LGBTQ+ parents call it beneficial	% of LGBTQ+ parents say 'Yes' it occurs	% of LGBTQ+ parents say 'No' it does not	% of LGBTQ+ parents 'Unsure'
Posters inclusive of LGBTQ+ parented families (e.g. books and posters)	95.9	95.9	19.3	53.51	27.19

Justifications:

- Preference for books and posters that reflect all forms of diversity in schools including ethnicity, multiculturalism, marriage status, pathways to parenthood including LGBTQ+ parents, rather than books and posters exclusively LGBTQ+ related.
- Signals a safe and inclusive school environment to parents and students.
- Encourages views that LGBTQ+ parents are 'normal' forms of family diversity.
- Potentially overcomes parent concerns about treatment post-disclosure in school contexts.
- Concerns may be a tokenistic support that does not influence how LGBTQ+ parents or their children are treated or supported by individuals in schools.

	% of LGBTQ+ parents call it important	% of LGBTQ+ parents call it beneficial	% of LGBTQ+ parents say 'Yes' it occurs	% of LGBTQ+ parents say 'No' it does not	% of LGBTQ+ parents 'Unsure'
Explicit mention of LGBTQ+ parent family formations in school websites and posters	86.3	90.4	14.78	50.43	34.78

Justifications:

- Signals a welcoming school environment and sets a clear stance of schools toward LGBTQ+ identities.
- Overcome parents' concerns about potential backlash to coming out in schools, including school events where both same-sex parents are present.
- Should be given the same explicit mention and included within current provisions for other family types and minority groups in schools. Or, developed to be inclusive of all forms of family structures and points of diversity.
- Raise awareness in school communities about people who may identify as LGBTQ+ including parents and students.
- Preference for explicit mention in school websites and documents when embedded within statements that protect other points of diversity such as ethnicity, multiculturalism, and family structures.

LGBTQ+ inclusive Curriculum (e.g., Lessons and books including LGBTQ+ Parents)	% of LGBTQ+ parents call it important	% of LGBTQ+ parents call it beneficial	% of LGBTQ+ parents say 'Yes' it occurs	% of LGBTQ+ parents say 'No' it does not	% of LGBTQ+ parents 'Unsure'
	80.8	88.7	8.85	61.95	29.2

Justifications:

- Potentially normalise LGBTQ+ parented families as one of many different types of family structures present in schools.
- Addresses parents' concerns about the lack of representation of LGBTQ+ parents in schools, and over-representation of dual-gendered traditional 'mother and father' structures.
- Raises school awareness of people who may identify as LGBTQ+ and addresses stereotypical beliefs or potential knowledge gaps identified in school community members (e.g., other parents, teachers and other students).
- Preference to be included within discussions about family structures generally rather than specific lessons that focus exclusively on LGBTQ+.

Overarching themes:

- LGBTQ+ related supports can signal safe environments for parents and overcome unique challenges such as disclosure in school contexts.
- Parents value school supports that discuss all forms of family diversity including LGBTQ+ family structures to normalise all family structures.
- Parents value teachers, schools and other members of the school community who are aware of LGBTQ+ parented families and offer equal treatment for all types of family structures.
- Parents have concern over backlash on purely LGBTQ+ foci, and on their family/selves.

features that support LGBTQ+ parents only. This study further indicates LGBTQ+ parented families desire to be perceived as only one of many different types of family structures in schools, rather than as a 'special case' of family diversity with unique supports specifically for the minority group. In part, this was linked to how parents had concerns around backlash to purely LGBTQ+ specific foci for inclusion efforts, and to their families and to their selves. This dominant ideal for schools' inclusion approaches reflects school guide research which argues that schools should embed LGBTQ+ parented families within current school practices, training and procedures to encourage the acknowledgement and representation of LGBTQ+ parents as *just one of many aspects of diversity* present in school contexts (UNESCO, 2016).

It is important to note that even a study *intentionally pitched* at revealing positive and supportive experiences in schools, school environments inclusive of diverse families were rare, as were the provision of LGBTQ+ related support features. This highlights that Australian schools may be similar to schools based in the US, which have similarly been found to have low rates of LGBTQ+ related school supports (Bishop & Atlas, 2015). The identified lack of supportive features in schools may not be surprising given the relative dearth of educational policies that explicitly mention LGBTQ+ parents, and considerable heated debate within Australian politics and media regarding how LGBTQ+ identities (if at all) should be included within Australian educational policies, procedures and practices (e.g. Safe Schools Coalition and Religious Freedom Review; Ferfolja & Ullman, 2017; Law, 2017).

The negative experiences discussed which included misperceptions of LGBTQ+ parents and the identified lack of supportive features in schools may also stem from the news media's role as many education stakeholders' first known exposure to LGBTQ+ parents and as a source for miseducation. Murdoch media in Australia – which dominates much of the news constructions of LGBTQ+ parenting and indeed most Australian news discourse – can be decidedly conservative and at times potentially considered a site for homophobic and transphobic material urging on 'moral panics' about LGBTQ+ people in education in articles and/or hosted comments sections online (Copland & Rasmussen, 2017; Law, 2017; Tomazin & Zhuang, 2019). News media about queer families has also been discussed in this book as more broadly reinforcing hetero-gendered norms and ideals for parents and families (Carlile & Paechter, 2018; Lynch & Morison, 2016). Invocations of both LGBTQ+ parent celebrities and everyday LGBTQ+ parents in news media political campaigns can suggest luxurious or wayward lifestyles which may invoke class, religious and other cultural sensitivities (Carlile & Paechter, 2018; Lynch & Morison, 2016). Another strong trope in all kinds of leftist, centrist and rightist leaning of Australian media coverage of LGBTQ+ parents has included arguments on 'the best interests of the child' of the married and coupled parent, which can create an inverse negative construction of solo, poly and divorced parents, for example, certainly felt by some participants in the study and expressed as a bias of schools in need of redress – reflecting wider theorising literature (Cubby, 2004; Hook, 2017; Von Doussa & Power, 2019).

Depictions of LGBTQ+ parents in children's popular culture (including books, movies, television serials, reality TV/ documentaries, and video games) which might be used as educational resources, have been regularly denounced in the Australian and international media as though they are exposing children to sexual topics – when really they are focussed on loving relationships and family relationships (Cubby, 2004). The data showed this broader denouncement of such resources as sexual, may be appropriated by some school community members themselves and applied to LGBTQ+ parents themselves engaging with their children at school drop-off or on play dates for example – as though the LGBTQ+ parent individual is themselves inherently sexual. Whilst the representations of LGBTQ+ parents in popular culture for adults themselves promote accounts neither completely normalising or pathologising these parents broadly (Riggs, 2011), the more solitary depictions of transgender parenting did seem reflected in some transgender parent participants' claims of being received and assumed as separate from other guardianship structures or as having an inactive parenting role. As news media and popular culture representations of LGBTQ+ parent can be influential in educational staff and society's perceptions or beliefs of LGBTQ+ parents generally, there is a need for more affirming, normalizing and complex representations given their potential influence on school contexts.

7.3 Most support was one-off, ad-hoc &/or 'unknown'

Despite highly charged social, political and religious debates regarding the 'controversial' inclusions of LGBTQ+ identities within schools, results from this study indicate LGBTQ+ parents particularly value amendments made to aspects of schools they are most often exposed to: teachers and school forms. Nonetheless, parents deemed all supportive school structures beneficial and important in creating more welcoming, tolerant and accepting school environments. Additionally, supportive structures were commonly justified as methods to overcome known challenges LGBTQ+ parented families face within school contexts including marginalisation, points of exclusion and lack of knowledge of diverse family structures in school community members (Lindsay et al., 2006). This places Australian schools in unique positions of authority having the ability to selectively develop and implement several supportive features within school environments deemed important and beneficial by LGBTQ+ parents. This may be particularly relevant to educational professionals and policymakers given the benefits of quality parent-school relationships to student outcomes (such as academic achievement; Henderson & Mapp, 2002) and educational policies' stress on including the perspective of parents in amending school policies, practices and procedures to be inclusive for diversity present in students and families (e.g., Australian Institute for Teaching and School Leadership/AITSL, 2011).

LGBTQ+ parents with children in Australian schools also noted schools provided supportive features differentially with some school contexts including more supportive structures than others. Commonly, LGBTQ+ parents were either unaware of or not receiving endorsed inclusive supports such as teachers trained to accommodate LGBTQ+ parented families, LGBTQ+ inclusive curriculums, and non-gendered language in school forms. Most parents had at least one affirming experience; however, these were one-offs such as accommodations on family-centric days (e.g. Mother's Day and Father's Day) or reliant on individual staff choice rather than systematically included in school systems. Schools should work on holistically embedding supportive structural and social features within educational contexts, and privileging the voices of LGBTQ+ parented families in how they would like to be included and represented in school environments. Specific supports most urgently endorsed by this sample included training of staff in LGBTQ+ family structures – which should be clearly announced by schools where it already occurs – and inclusive school forms. Inclusive school forms may be a particularly viable supportive feature within school contexts given the relatively low amount of time and cost required to implement the support compared to inclusive teacher training endeavours. However, whilst constituting an easy first step, the reason why inclusive school forms are so valued is that they hint at broader structural and social inclusive school characteristics and features that should also be worked towards.

Australian news media has likely contributed to all kinds of education stakeholders' lack of education law and policy knowledge around the endorsed provisions and supports for LGBTQ+ parented families; though the media has *often* focussed on issues of education law and policy on LGBTQ+ people in hundreds of articles (Law, 2017; Tomazin & Zhuang, 2019). It has at times however achieved this focus through ignoring or politicising, and outrightly questioning the application of many relevant policy protections for LGBTQ+ people in its broader conservative political campaigns whilst inciting 'moral panics' about schools and LGBTQ+ people (Law, 2017; Tomazin & Zhuang, 2019). This has been achieved in ways that may be making readers imagine the protection for LGBTQ+ people *that does exist* either does not, should not, or would be inadequate against the imagined pervasive resistance to the protections these texts appear to fabricate... Given that most Australians voted for same-sex marriage, it can be extrapolated such anti-LGBTQ+ feeling is perhaps exaggerated. At times such Australian media has been arguably misrepresenting the details of policies and programs in educational spaces to incite division and influence elections, rather than taking seriously the responsibility to inform the public on legislative and policy updates affecting them in straightforward educational ways (Copland & Rasmussen, 2017; Law, 2017; Tomazin & Zhuang, 2019). Politicising media can be in this sense, failing both LGBTQ+ parents and other school stakeholders on issues of accurately communicating current education policy in a bias-free and informational way, alongside failing to support the inclusion needs of LGBTQ+ people (especially students) in schools more broadly (Law, 2017; Tomazin & Zhuang, 2019).

7.4 'Business-as-usual' low-fuss pluralistic inclusion model ideal

A dominant theme throughout qualitative analysis of parents' arguments for the inclusion of school supports indicated a preference for models of inclusion that accommodated all potential points of family and individual diversity, rather than focussing on LGBTQ+ families or issues as a distinct and unique topic or form of family diversity. Parents particularly valued school approaches to inclusivity that did not endorse traditional assumptions of nuclear dual-gendered family structures and instead focussed on pluralistic and unpredictable diversity in all school structures, in a proactive way. Schools should, in this view, question school practices, procedures and practices that endorse and assume 'normal and expected' (only white, only heterosexual, only cisgender, only male and so forth) forms of identity in students and their families. Schools should also develop and implement structural supports (e.g. school policy on parent-school relationships, anti-bullying policy, diversity statements, further training in educational professionals) that accommodate a variety of potential differences in students including diverse ethnicities, cultures, sexual orientations, gender identities and family structures including single, divorced, married, foster, intergenerational and other types of parent/ guardian relationships.

This finding builds on US research finding that LGBTQ+ parents' value 'Business-As-Usual' mindsets and pluralist views of family diversity, where LGBTQ+ parented families are offered the same treatment and accommodations as other families within school communities (Bower, 2008; Goldberg et al., 2017). However, school policy (AITSL, 2011) and research (Riggs & Willing, 2013) suggest that parents are required to 'come out' or disclose their sexual orientation and/or gender identity to schools and teachers to receive desired equal treatment and acknowledgement. This may prove challenging for LGBTQ+ parents as they may not all reside in contexts that are safe or welcoming to such disclosures. They can depend on environmental factors such as legal protections, cultural beliefs, educational policy, media, local community, school ethos, and educational professional stance and views toward LGBTQ+ adults, couples and parents (Botha et al., 2020). Parents in less affirming legal frameworks and cultural or societal views of LGBTQ+ identities have noted concerns in 'coming out' to school and family health professionals including potential backlash to themselves and their children, the potential involvement of family welfare services, and lack of acknowledgement of parents that are not legally or biologically related to their children (Lindsay et al., 2006; Shields et al., 2012). More research is needed in diverse legal, social and cultural frameworks to explore parent experiences in schools as most research has been drawn from lesbian female cis-gendered mothers with high incomes residing in inner-metropolitan locations with at least some legal protections for LGBTQ+ adults and parents.

The valuing of pluralism or being accommodated, recognised and framed as one of many different forms of family diversity indicates LGBTQ+ parents would like inclusive practices, procedures and policies to be embedded within current protections for multicultural, single, blended, married, divorced, intergenerational, foster/adoptive and other forms of family diversity. This dominant theme of equal treatment and recognition of all forms of diversity contrasts against recent highly visible debates in politics, the public and media regarding 'if and how' LGBTQ+ individual's, couples and parents should be protected and included in legal systems, school environments, family health and other services (Australian Bureau of Statistics/ABS, 2017; Law, 2017). Legislative protections are an important first step to the recognition and acknowledgement of LGBTQ+ couples and parents, but may not coincide with more affirming views in social and cultural contexts (Botha et al., 2020). This may be the case in Australia as national samples indicate a divisive split in the population with around 60% supporting (and 40% opposing) the legalisation of marriage equality (ABS, 2017), which had location-based trends.

Given not all LGBTQ+ parents are 'out' within school environments and parents may fear adverse reactions to disclosure of LGBTQ+ identity in school contexts (Lindsay et al., 2006), a proactive Business-As-Usual model should foreground overcoming a range of unique barriers LGBTQ+ and other parents experience within school contexts, including gaps in teacher professional knowledge of family diversity and creating informed school communities for LGBTQ+ parented families' intended or unintended disclosures, but without requiring or only responding to performances of 'outness' or 'pride' – which are simply not always possible or preferable for LGBTQ+ people.

This proposed model appears to some degree aligned with national policy topics on the need to respect and understand family diversity in the school community – particularly seen in the *Family-School Partnerships: A Guide for Schools and Families* (Department of Education, Employment and Workplace Relations, 2019). The 'Business-As-Usual' Low-fuss Pluralistic Inclusion Model is especially aligned with policy topics seen in Tasmanian *Guidelines for Supporting Sexual and Gender Diversities in Schools and Colleges* (Tasmanian Department of Education, 2012), including the emphasis on school community members upholding acceptance and understanding of LGBT status as being another form of 'normal' diversity. It is also in some alignment with Victorian policy suggested strategies on ensuring school policies, practices, procedures, and curriculum are inclusive of family diversity in the *Framework for Improving Student Outcomes* (Department of Education Victoria, 2019). It loosely fits Queensland and Australian Capital Territory provisions on the cultural diversity of families or diversity broadly (ACT Government, 2018; Queensland Government, 2019). It also loosely fits some of the South Australian and Western Australian guidelines for supporting sexual and gender diversity in schools (Department for Education and Child Development, 2016; Equal Opportunity Commission of Western Australia, 2013). However, there is room for further highlighting the potential for the approach in these policies and resourcing the rollout of the approach in all of these states in much more detail given this approach has yet to be experienced at the ground level to its full potential. The model is aligned to a much smaller extent with New South Wales and

Northern Territory provisions for differentiated support for community or family, and students – though these provisions may need some added expansions and enumerations to be effective in promoting and resourcing the approach.

7.5 Geographic transferability & temporal relics

Aspects of these findings may be transferable internationally. The introductory chapter showed that Europe and the Americas, which are more strongly impacted by regional networking through rights-based polity and health networks, have many more protections in place impacting LGBTQ+ parents that are commensurate with the Australian context (Botha et al., 2020; Jones, 2019). Thus LGBTQ+ parents' preferencing for a 'Business-As-Usual' approach in Australia may be worth consideration in some of these other policy-protected contexts and also to individual policy-protected countries from elsewhere with similar cultures around LGBTQ+ issues such as New Zealand, South Africa, Israel, Japan and Taiwan. However, it is also important to note that there may be other local nuances in play that lend emphasis to different discourses. For example, South Africa's embrace of diversity has especially benefited from the notion of human rights discourses in the public domain post-Apartheid, whereas family constructions of LGBTQ+ people in the private realm can be more problematic, and this may influence the best ways to include LGBTQ+ parents in that context towards drawing on relevant local visions for rights and local rights histories so important to education as part of public life in South Africa (Francis et al., 2018; Jones, 2018).

However, even in countries with legal recognition for LGBTQ+ parents and families where the 'Business-As-Usual' model will have value, LGBTQ+ parents' experiences of minority stress do not automatically end when legal equality sets in (Siegel et al., 2021). Schools should understand the possible lingering effects of legal vulnerability on LGBTQ+ parents in protected contexts: perceived unequal relationship recognition creating the sense one or one's relations are treated as "second-class" by the school; adverse mental health outcomes as relics of past legal vulnerability on the individual level such as anxieties about how the school community may view parental legitimacy, or on the family level such as continuance of perceived unequal relationship recognition and related secrecies about family members (LeBlanc et al., 2015; Siegel et al., 2021). These issues may perpetuate tensions and anxieties around education spaces even where no specific homophobic or transphobic messaging or treatment and active inclusion occurs.

The perceptions of older, religious or ethnically/culturally diverse LG-BTQ+ parents and those with other intersectional factors enhancing a sense of outsider status from queer rights movements and homonormativity, may be particularly sensitised to any microaggressions or lack of welcome (divorcees, solo parents (Hook, 2017; Von Doussa & Power, 2019). This perception should not be denied or dismissed where it arises; it should be understood in context and handled with sensitivity and long-term ongoing efforts to show that 'Business-As-Usual' is going to now include a *better kind* of 'business' for a *broader* 'usual'.

Conversely, LGBTQ+ parents in countries lacking policy protection particularly in Africa, Asia and Oceania; and in certain Eastern European contexts such as Russia or Poland for example where homophobic and transphobic notions around families have been perpetuated by various propaganda efforts, may simply have other more urgent concerns than just being treated the same as everyone else in their school system. Legal vulnerability constitutes an increased risk for parental and child health in these contexts as well as family functioning through individual and shared pathways between family members (Siegel et al., 2021). Issues of safety, issues of economic security and therefore needs for privacy may be more strongly and immediately valued by LGBTQ+ parents in these contexts, including LGBTQ+ 'outing' options on forms could be seen as exposing people to government surveillance or punitive measures for example. There may be ways of including all relevant parents on forms by just adding names under 'emergency contacts' without demanding information on roles and relations (as one example).

Evidence from the small number of reviews of unprotected contexts for LGBTQ+ parents further suggests that at an individual level, family members engage in person-centered counteractions to their conditions like emotion regulation, researching legal information on how best to protect their family or what positive legal change in other countries may become possible in their own and how, or in querying heteronormativity within legislation and family models (Dalton & Bielby, 2000; Kazyak et al., 2018; Ollen & Goldberg, 2016; Siegel et al., 2021). These efforts can be aided by lesson content in some contexts, confidential psychological support services available to all extended family members and emergency contacts in others, in both direct and indirect ways. Extra emphasis on the importance of never requiring outness and emphasising safety and privacy concerns would be key. Some aspects of the Business-As-Usual model may here be useful, such as a general effort to de-centre the heteronormative family in indirect ways across structures and language without ever replacing it with (or in certain contexts where it is dangerous, naming) any other specific type of family. The application needs to be relative to context, but there exists no context in which a flag of hope and inclusion cannot be upraised – if even just in indirect ways or in efforts at extending a sense of care and protection towards all school community members.

7.6 Summary of key points

Overall, the main learnings from this book include:

- National/state laws, educational policies, research and public views, protections, and punishments toward LGBTQ+ adults, couples and parents can differ.
- Schools and public services can be challenging for LGBTQ+ parents when they encounter people and practices that assume all family structures are 'traditional' and have dual-gendered (Mother and Father) family constellations.
- There is little guidance for teachers and schools in 'if and how' LGBTQ+ parents should be included in schools. But, parents value schools and teachers that treat all different types of family structures and ethnicities equally.
- Parents particularly valued educational professionals trained in LGBTQ+ forms of family diversity, and school enrolment forms and communications that did not use gendered language (e.g. Mothers and Fathers, vs. parents, carers and families).

LGBTQ+ parents valued teachers who view their families as one of many forms of family diversity, are knowledgeable about LGBTQ+ family constellations, and are comfortable in discussing LGBTQ+ topics or issues in schools. This requires the inclusion of these concepts in teacher education programs and professional development workshops. Such training could also pass on that parents also value sensitive pedagogy in lessons focussed on families including careful wording around gender and parents, and adapting lessons that may exclude LGBTQ+ parented children – such as creating classrooms where it is completely supported for students to be crafting two gifts for parents on Mother's or Father's day or for other types of important guardians in their lives.

Parents value both classroom and broader schooling environments that represent a wide range of family types (e.g. intergenerational, step, blended, single, married, defacto and LGBTQ+) in posters, books and lessons – this is going to be more easily achieved by schools where it is policy-supported and leadership-led and endorsed at the highest levels but may also realistically need to be promoted by education leaders and staff working in any level of education systems. LGBTQ+ parents' ideal for school forms is those that use non-gendered language (e.g. parent or carer) over gendered language (e.g. mother and father). They also more broadly value mention of LGBTQ+ families in school websites and documents when included alongside other forms of diversity (e.g. different family constellations, race/ethnicity. The chapter showed the valuing of LGBTQ+ supportive curricula has likely been in some ways miscast by politicising media environments; both LGBTQ+ parents and schools should be very careful to pay more attention to the law and policy than news outlets that run anti-LGBTQ+ features; and not to throw the proverbial gayby-baby students' needs out with the media's hyped and sensationalising bathwater.

7.7 Implications for educational stakeholders

This study's findings have clear implications for education stakeholders in contexts including and like Australia where LGBTQ+ parents have some level of legal and policy protections in place. These include implications for politicians and policymakers, university teacher educators, schools, educational professionals, and researchers. Although, it is important to note these strategies may not be practical options or applicable in different legal, social and cultural frameworks.

7.7.1 Politicians and policymakers

LGBTQ+ parents value being viewed and treated as just one of many different forms of diversity in school communities. They desire school policy contexts that treat them as a non-issue or Business-As-Usual. They do not value stand-alone 'add-ons' provisions that treat LGBTQ+ parents as different or separate from others and desire schools that view and accommodate LGBTQ+ parents in similar ways to other points of diversity including ethnicity, other family constellations (e.g. single, married, divorced, inter-generational, foster). They experience school contexts that include misinformed assumptions and stereotypical beliefs about LGBTQ+ identities generally, and value school communities that are informed and aware of all potential forms of family diversity in schools. School practices deemed important to parents included:

- pre- and in-service professional development in LGBTQ+ families embedded alongside other family structures (e.g. intergenerational, single, married, divorced, blended, foster, adoptive and other), and

- school communications and enrolment forms that used inclusive non-gendered language.

Schools can differ in 'if and how' they approach LGBTQ+ identities, despite the recent changes to legislative rights. There is a need for the development of policy and research targeted to meet the unique needs of LGBTQ+ parents and schools, may need to 'proactively approach' the development of such policy to meet professional quality standards of care. Community NGOs in Australia have similarly argued the need for standardised training in LGBTQ+ public services (Hill et al., 2020). United Nations educational policy development frameworks for the LGBTQ+ school community and minority groups should be consulted (UNESCO, 2013, 2016).

7.7.2 *University teacher educators*

LGBTQ+ parents find professional educators with negative and uninformed beliefs about LGBTQ+ identities a potential barrier in forming quality parent-school relationships. Parents value educational professionals who are informed about LGBTQ+ family constellations and accommodate all forms of family diversity (e.g. single, blended, divorced, married, multicultural, etc.) equally. Teacher educators and professional development providers should include professional content on LGBTQ+ parented families alongside other forms of diversity present in school communities such as multiculturalism and English as a second language. Such training should particularly focus on material that (UNESCO, 2016):

- is informative, evidence-based and reflective allowing educators to address their own attitudes and beliefs toward people who may identify as LGBTQ+,
- has been developed in collaboration with LGBTQ+ NGOs and parent groups,
- is embedded within the training that includes and represents all types of family structures.

7.7.3 *Schools*

Schools can treat LGBTQ+ parents differently, with little explicit policy advising 'if and how' LGBTQ+ parents should be included in schools. LGBTQ+ parents valued being treated the same as any other type of family structure. Parents deemed teacher professional development in LGBTQ+ family structures as important and beneficial in creating welcoming school contexts; and school enrolment forms and communications that focused on relationships to children (e.g., parent/carer/guardian, dear families, etc.).

Recommendations for schools include (UNESCO, 2016):

- explore educational policy regarding parent-school relationships as justification for including LGBTQ+ inclusive supports in schools,
- review and update school practices and procedures that unintentionally exclude LGBTQ+ parents such as school enrolment forms,
- source professional development and consult with NGOS that focus on family diversity including LGBTQ+ parents.

7.7.4 School educators

LGBTQ+ parents encourage mindfulness within teachers in creating inclusive classroom environments including careful language use, differentiation of lessons to include/reflect diverse family structures and competent professional knowledge of diverse family structures. These include:

- open informed discussions around LGBTQ+ parented families as one of many types of family diversity,
- the representation of LGBTQ+ parents alongside other forms of diversity in classroom materials and learning activities,
- collaborative and respectful relationships between parents and schools around 'how' they would like to be included in school contexts,
- non-gendered language in school forms addressing parents and families,
- teachers who are aware, competent and appreciative about a wide range of potential points of diversity in school communities (e.g. ethnicity, single, blended family structures, etc.).

7.7.5 Researchers

More research is needed from the perspective of a multitude of school stakeholders regarding the question 'if and how' LGBTQ+ parents should be included in schools including teachers, parents, school leadership, educational policymakers, legal professionals to name a few. Australian research exploring LGBTQ+ parent experiences in schools is particularly thick in qualitative research that over-represents lesbian

Caucasian mothers of high socio-economic backgrounds in early childhood contexts. Further research is needed to explore the perspective of other potential intersections such as low socio-economic status, other LGBTQ+ identities and diverse ethnicities. There is also a need for further quantitative research in larger samples to explore the rate, frequency and trend of parents' positive and negative experiences in schools. Such measurements should be aligned to current data sets (e.g. parent satisfaction with schools) already gathered by national, state or school levels to allow comparison using statistical analysis.

We note a lot of the advice covered here may not be necessarily transferrable in direct ways in some more punitive countries within Africa, Europe and/or Asia for example where the laws may be quite different for LGBTQ+ parents and safety may be an even more primary concern. It will be important therefore for local researchers to look into locally relevant nuances, needs and strategies – and for international rights bodies and research collaborators to support them in doing so as needed. However, the advice to schools and teachers wishing to support rainbow families in these environments to cover curricula in ways supportive of a diversity of families in general (with or without direct mention of LGBTQ+ families depending on contextual constraints and possibilities), may still be useful and supported in some countries' laws and policies, and may be a way to contribute to environments where LGBTQ+ diversities nonetheless exist and require support even if indirect as necessary – that researchers should consider and explore.

7.7.6 *Other stakeholders*

Media and popular culture creatives should provide more incidental coverage of diverse LGBTQ+ parents in affirming ways within discussions of other education topics (where parents are not problematised/politicised) at the Macrosystem level in media and popular culture would assist Australian and other parents, re-shaping ideas in their school Microsystems. Resistant coverage of LGBTQ+ parents de-gendering parenthood in school contexts and valorising queer parenting in school events could challenge the cis/heteronormative gold standard school parent (to build on more general work of Lynch & Morison, 2016).

7.8 Conclusion

Schools differ in the provision of LGBTQ+ related school supports, despite these supports being highly valued by most LGBTQ+ parents. Parents highlighted similar challenging experiences in schools reported in research in the early 2000s (Lindsay et al., 2006), strengthening arguments that schools are slow to adapt to social and legal changes (Robinson, 2002). Legal amendments (like marriage equality) do not correlate directly with changes in cultural, social and public service views toward LGBTQ+ adults, couples and parents (Botha et al., 2020). Media and popular culture depictions of LGBTQ+ parents, and other cultural and social factors including religions, may influence conditions. However, given the recent changes in Australian national laws, and schools' differential stances to the inclusion of LGBTQ+ parents, there is an evident need to develop more standardised and systematic methods of inclusion to meet 'quality service' standards and benchmarks. This book highlighted a range of phenomena that schools and policy developers should avoid including:

- school policies, practices and procedures that assume all families in schools are parented by cis-gendered, heterosexual adults legally and biologically related to children,
- assumptions that all educational professionals are supportive of LGBTQ+ parented families,
- reactive measures of support that require parents and caretakers to disclose their family diversity, sexual orientation or gender identity for inclusive teaching practices,
- treating LGBTQ+ families as 'unusual' in highly visible, exclusive supports.

LGBTQ+ parents offered a *clear vision* for their desired support – favouring a holistic centring of assumptions of pluralist family diversities in school structures, social engagements, resources and materials such that many differences would be understood as within the broad expectation of 'Business-As-Usual'. They encouraged staff training on professional duties around family diversities, inclusive forms allowing diverse family constellations and arrangements, assumptions of diversities as a background to everyday lesson content and engagements, and diverse representation of families in books and materials including *but not limited to* LGBTQ+ parented families. Moving into the future, greater examination of LGBTQ+ parents' experiences of new supports that emerge, and LGBTQ+ parents' progressive confidence in increasing what can be imagined and achieved in schools, will help build our understanding of what works best to support them.

References

ABS. (2017). *1800.0 - Australian Marriage Law Postal Survey, 2017.* Retrieved from https://www.abs.gov.au/websitedbs/D3310114.nsf/home/AMLPS+-+Privacy+Policy

ACT Government. (2018). *Strategic Plan 2018–21.* Canberra: ACT Education Directorate.

AITSL. (2011). *Australian Professional Standards for Teachers.* Canberra: AITSL.

Bishop, C. M., & Atlas, J. G. (2015). School curriculum, policies, and practices regarding lesbian, gay, bisexual, and transgender families. *Education and Urban Society, 47*(7), 766–784.

Botha, K., Lelis, R., López De La Peña, E., & Tan, D. (2020). *State-Sponsored Homophobia Global Legislation Overview.* Retrieved from https://ilga.org/downloads/ILGA_World_State_Sponsored_Homophobia_report_global_legislation_overview_update_December_2020.pdf

Carlile, A., & Paechter, C. (2018). *LGBTQI Parented Families and Schools.* London: Routledge.

Copland, S., & Rasmussen, M. L. (2017). Safe schools, marriage equality and LGBT youth suicide. In T. Jones (Ed.), *Bent Street.* Melbourne: Clouds of Magellan Press.

Cubby, B. (2004). Play School's lesbian tale sparks outrage. *Sydney Morning Herald.* Retrieved from https://www.smh.com.au/national/play-schools-lesbian-tale-sparks-outrage-20040604-gdj23z.html

Dalton, S., & Bielby, D. (2000). That's our kind of constellation. *Gender & Society, 14*(1), 36–61.

Department for Education and Child Development. (2016). *Wellbeing for Learning and Life.* Adelaide: SA Government.

Department of Education, Employment and Workplace Relations. (2019). *Family-School Partnerships Framework.* Canberra: ACT Australian Government.

Department of Education Victoria. (2019). *Framework for Improving Student Outcomes.* Melbourne: Victorian Government.

Equal Opportunity Commission of Western Australia. (2013). *Guidelines for Supporting Sexual and Gender Diversity in Schools.* Perth: WAEOC.

Ferfolja, T., & Ullman, J. (2017). Gender and sexuality in education and health: voices advocating for equity and social justice. *Sex Education, 17*(3), 235–241.

Fox, R. K. (2007). One of the Hidden diversities in schools. *Childhood Education, 83*(5), 277–281.

Francis, D., Reygan, F., Brown, A., Dlamini, B., McAllister, J., Nogela, L., … Thani, G. (2018). A five country study of gender and sexuality diversity and schooling in Southern Africa. *Africa Education Review, 16*, 1–21.

Goldberg, A. E., Black, K., Sweeney, K., & Moyer, A. (2017). Lesbian, gay, and heterosexual adoptive parents' perceptions of inclusivity and receptiveness

152   *Summary and conclusions*

in early childhood education settings. *Journal of Research in Childhood Education, 31*(1), 141–159.

Henderson, A., & Mapp, K. (2002). *A New Wave of Evidence.* Austin: Southwest Educational Development Laboratory.

Hill, A. O., Bourne, A., McNair, R., Carman, M., & Lyons, A. (2020). *Private Lives 3.* Melbourne: ARCSHS.

Hook, G. (2017). The child's best interests? In T. Jones (Ed.), *Bent Street* (Vol. 2017, pp. 26–33). Melbourne: Clouds of Magellan.

Jones, T. (2018). South African contributions to LGBTI education issues. *Sex Education, 19*(4), 455–471.

Jones, T. (2019). Legal Landscapes. In T. Jones, L. Coll, L. van Leent, & Y. Taylor (Eds.), *Uplifting Gender and Sexuality Education Research* (pp. 87–112). Basingstoke: Palgrave Macmillan.

Kazyak, E., Woodell, B., Scherrer, K., & Finken, E. (2018). Law and family formation among LGBQ-parent families. *Family Court Review, 56*(1), 364–373.

Law, B. (2017). Moral Panic 101. *Quarterly Essay, 1*(67), 1–19.

LeBlanc, A., Frost, D., & Wight, R. (2015). Minority stress and stress proliferation among same-sex and other marginalized couples. *Journal of Marriage Family Practice, 77*(1), 40–59.

Lindsay, J., Perlesz, A., Brown, R., McNair, R., De Vaus, D., & Pitts, M. (2006). Stigma or respect. *Sociology, 40*(6), 1059–1077.

Lynch, I., & Morison, T. (2016). Gay men as parents. *Feminism & Psychology, 26,* 188–206.

Ollen, E., & Goldberg, A. (2016). Parent-child conversations about legal inequalities in gay- and lesbian-parent families in Florida. *Journal of GLBT Family Studies, 12*(1), 365–385.

Queensland Government. (2019). *Advancing Partnerships.* Brisbane: Queensland Government.

Riggs, D. W. (2011). Let's go to the movies. *Journal of GLBT Family Studies, 7*(3), 297–312.

Riggs, D. W., & Willing, I. (2013). They're all just little bits, aren't they. *Journal of Australian Studies, 37*(3), 364–377.

Robinson, K. H. (2002). Making the invisible visible. *Contemporary Issues in Early Childhood, 3*(3), 415–434.

Shields, L., Zappia, T., Blackwood, D., Watkins, R., Wardrop, J., & Chapman, R. (2012). Lesbian, gay, bisexual, and transgender parents seeking health care for their children. *Worldviews on Evidence-Based Nursing, 9*(4), 200–209.

Siegel, M., Assenmacher, C., Meuwly, N., & Zemp, M. (2021). The legal vulnerability model for same-sex parent families: A mixed methods systematic review and theoretical integration. *Frontiers in Psychology, 12,* 1–28.

Tasmanian Department of Education. (2012). Guidelines for Supporting Sexual and Gender Diversity in Schools and Colleges. Hobart: Tasmanian Government.

Tomazin, F., & Zhuang, Y. (2019). Safe Schools scare campaign targets Chinese-Australian voters. *Sydney Morning Herald.* Retrieved from https://

www.smh.com.au/federal-election-2019/safe-schools-scare-campaign-targets-chinese-australian-voters-20190427-p51hrk.html

UNESCO. (2013). UNESCO Handbook on Education policy analysis and programming, volume 1. *UNESCO Digital Library*, *1*, 1–92.

UNESCO. (2016). *Out In The Open*. UNESCO: Paris.

Von Doussa, H., & Power, J. (2019). A lesson in queer. In T. Jones (Ed.), *Bent Street* (Vol. 2). Melbourne: Clouds of Magellan.

Glossary

Androgynous Can mean having both masculine and feminine characteristics or having neither specifically masculine nor feminine characteristics. People with intersex variations may sometimes be androgynous. Some people who are androgynous may identify as genderqueer, trans or androgynous.

Asexual People without strong sexual attraction or desire, regardless of their romantic orientation or sexual behaviour.

Bisexual or Bi People whose sexual or romantic feelings can be for men and women.

Cisgender/ed Refers to people whose internal sense of gender and/or sex matches the sex they were assigned at birth.

Gay/lesbian/homosexual People whose sexual and romantic feelings are primarily for the same sex.

Gender Expression The enaction of gender-related identity such as through self-presentation, clothing and/or behaviours.

Gender Identity The gender-related identity, appearance or mannerisms, or other gender-related characteristics of an individual (whether by way of medical intervention or not, socialisation or alternative expression), with or without regard to the individual's designated sex at birth.

Genderqueer/non-binary People who do not socially comply with traditional male or female gender expectations through their dress, hair, mannerisms, appearance and values.

LGBTQ+/LGBTIQ+ Lesbian, gay, bisexual, transgender and otherwise queer/questioning (people). Sometimes formally includes intersex (the I), where relevant and appropriate. In this book we explored LGBTQ+ peoples' experiences, but there were no participants reporting intersex variations.

Pansexual or Omnisexual   People whose sexual and romantic feelings are for people of any sex/gender; rejecting the gender binary of male/female only models.

Parent/guardian   Person in a formal caretaking and rearing role for a child/children (of any age). This can include people for example with a biological, social and/or legal relationship.

Queer   Queer is an anti-identity rejecting restrictive normative notions of strict consistent sexual orientations.

School   An educational institution whether run by government, religious or other independent bodies.

Sex   Sex is commonly expressed as a binary and used to divide people into males and females. However, in reality, sex is a complex relationship of genetic, hormonal, morphological, biochemical, and anatomical differences which variably impact both the physiology of the body and the sexual differentiation of the brain. Although everyone is assigned a sex at birth, researchers argue that approximately 2–4% percent of the population have an intersex variation.

Sexual Orientation   The direction of one's sexual and romantic attractions and interests towards members of the same, opposite or both sexes or all genders. Similar to 'Sexual Preference'.

Trans/Transgender   A broad umbrella term, including people/a person who identifies as a gender different to the one assigned at birth and who may or may not choose to undergo sex affirmation/ reassignment surgery(ies). Describes a broad range of nonconforming gender identities and/or behaviours.

Transition or Sex Affirmation   Refers to the process of socially, physically and/or legally changing or affirming ones' gender presentation/sex to some extent (whether slightly through to wholly). This process can involve changing how the person refers to/sees themselves, dresses or presents themselves (hairstyle and so forth), is referred to/seen by others (pronouns like he/she/they) and/or changing one's social role or role in relationships if relevant. It might also involve changing one's body through hormonal therapies/cosmetic procedures/a range of surgeries, and/or changing the way one is identified by sex on legal or reporting documents (birth certificate, passport, license and records).

Index